OPPOSING VIEWPOINTS® SERIES

Teens and Social Media

Other Books of Related Interest

Opposing Viewpoints Series

The #MeToo Movement
Cancel Culture
The New Censorship

At Issue Series

Does the Internet Increase Anxiety?
Trial by Internet
When Is Free Speech Hate Speech?

Current Controversies Series

America's Mental Health Crisis
Big Tech and Democracy
Privacy and Security in the Digital Age

> "Congress shall make no law … abridging the freedom of speech, or of the press."
>
> *First Amendment to the U.S. Constitution*

The basic foundation of our democracy is the First Amendment guarantee of freedom of expression. The Opposing Viewpoints series is dedicated to the concept of this basic freedom and the idea that it is more important to practice it than to enshrine it.

OPPOSING
VIEWPOINTS®
SERIES

Teens and Social Media

Gary Wiener, Book Editor

GREENHAVEN
PUBLISHING

Published in 2023 by Greenhaven Publishing, LLC
2544 Clinton Street,
Buffalo NY 14224

First Edition

Articles in Greenhaven Publishing anthologies are often edited for length to meet page requirements. In addition, original titles of these works are changed to clearly present the main thesis and to explicitly indicate the author's opinion. Every effort is made to ensure that Greenhaven Publishing accurately reflects the original intent of the authors. Every effort has been made to trace the owners of the copyrighted material.

Cover image: A_B_C/Shutterstock.com

Library of Congress Cataloging-in-Publication Data

Names: Wiener, Gary.
Title:Teens and social media / Gary Wiener (compiling editor)
Description: New York : Greenhaven, 2023. | Series: Opposing viewpoints| Includes bibliographic references and index.
Identifiers: ISBN 9781534509115 (pbk) | ISBN 9781534509122 (library bound)
Subjects: LCSH: Cyberbullying-- Juvenile literature | Mental health--Juvenile literature | Privacy-- Juvenile literature | Responsibility-- Juvenile literature | Social media-- Juvenile literature| Young adults (teenagers)-- Juvenile literature
Classification: LCC HQ799.2 M35 W54 2023 | DDC 302.23/1--dc23

Manufactured in the United States of America

Website: http://greenhavenpublishing.com

Contents

The Importance of Opposing Viewpoints

Perhaps every generation experiences a period in time in which the populace seems especially polarized, starkly divided on the important issues of the day and gravitating toward the far ends of the political spectrum and away from a consensus-facilitating middle ground. The world that today's students are growing up in and that they will soon enter into as active and engaged citizens is deeply fragmented in just this way. Issues relating to terrorism, immigration, women's rights, minority rights, race relations, health care, taxation, wealth and poverty, the environment, policing, military intervention, the proper role of government—in some ways, perennial issues that are freshly and uniquely urgent and vital with each new generation—are currently roiling the world.

If we are to foster a knowledgeable, responsible, active, and engaged citizenry among today's youth, we must provide them with the intellectual, interpretive, and critical-thinking tools and experience necessary to make sense of the world around them and of the all-important debates and arguments that inform it. After all, the outcome of these debates will in large measure determine the future course, prospects, and outcomes of the world and its peoples, particularly its youth. If they are to become successful members of society and productive and informed citizens, students need to learn how to evaluate the strengths and weaknesses of someone else's arguments, how to sift fact from opinion and fallacy, and how to test the relative merits and validity of their own opinions against the known facts and the best possible available information. The landmark series Opposing Viewpoints has been providing students with just such critical-thinking skills and exposure to the debates surrounding society's most urgent contemporary issues for many years, and it continues to serve this essential role with undiminished commitment, care, and rigor.

The key to the series's success in achieving its goal of sharpening students' critical-thinking and analytic skills resides in its title—

Opposing Viewpoints. In every intriguing, compelling, and engaging volume of this series, readers are presented with the widest possible spectrum of distinct viewpoints, expert opinions, and informed argumentation and commentary, supplied by some of today's leading academics, thinkers, analysts, politicians, policy makers, economists, activists, change agents, and advocates. Every opinion and argument anthologized here is presented objectively and accorded respect. There is no editorializing in any introductory text or in the arrangement and order of the pieces. No piece is included as a "straw man," an easy ideological target for cheap point-scoring. As wide and inclusive a range of viewpoints as possible is offered, with no privileging of one particular political ideology or cultural perspective over another. It is left to each individual reader to evaluate the relative merits of each argument—as he or she sees it, and with the use of ever-growing critical-thinking skills—and grapple with his or her own assumptions, beliefs, and perspectives to determine how convincing or successful any given argument is and how the reader's own stance on the issue may be modified or altered in response to it.

This process is facilitated and supported by volume, chapter, and selection introductions that provide readers with the essential context they need to begin engaging with the spotlighted issues, with the debates surrounding them, and with their own perhaps shifting or nascent opinions on them. In addition, guided reading and discussion questions encourage readers to determine the authors' point of view and purpose, interrogate and analyze the various arguments and their rhetoric and structure, evaluate the arguments' strengths and weaknesses, test their claims against available facts and evidence, judge the validity of the reasoning, and bring into clearer, sharper focus the reader's own beliefs and conclusions and how they may differ from or align with those in the collection or those of their classmates.

Research has shown that reading comprehension skills improve dramatically when students are provided with compelling, intriguing, and relevant "discussable" texts. The subject matter of these collections could not be more compelling, intriguing, or urgently relevant to today's students and the world they are poised to inherit. The anthologized articles and the reading and discussion questions that are included with them also provide the basis for stimulating, lively, and passionate classroom debates. Students who are compelled to anticipate objections to their own argument and identify the flaws in those of an opponent read more carefully, think more critically, and steep themselves in relevant context, facts, and information more thoroughly. In short, using discussable text of the kind provided by every single volume in the Opposing Viewpointsseries encourages close reading, facilitates reading comprehension, fosters research, strengthens critical thinking, and greatly enlivens and energizes classroom discussion and participation. The entire learning process is deepened, extended, and strengthened.

For all of these reasons, Opposing Viewpoints continues to be exactly the right resource at exactly the right time—when we most need to provide readers with the critical-thinking tools and skills that will not only serve them well in school but also in their careers and their daily lives as decision-making family members, community members, and citizens. This series encourages respectful engagement with and analysis of opposing viewpoints and fosters a resulting increase in the strength and rigor of one's own opinions and stances. As such, it helps make readers "future ready," and that readiness will pay rich dividends for the readers themselves, for the citizenry, for our society, and for the world at large.

Introduction

> *"While a few researchers have claimed that digital technology is a powerful, causal factor in the rising rates of mental health problems, others have countered that the risk of harm for most teenagers is tiny—about the equivalent influence on well-being as wearing eyeglasses or regularly eating potatoes."*
>
> *—Virginia Hughes, The New York Times*[1]

Given the current ubiquity of social media and the outsized role that it plays in the social lives of a majority of teens on the planet, it may seem hard to believe that social media platforms as we now know them are only about two decades old. Though there were forerunners (e.g. Friendster) to the current crop of social media sites, MySpace and LinkedIn were not launched until 2003. For a while, MySpace dominated the social media landscape; its focus on music attracted the young adult demographic. That it was rapidly replaced by Facebook shows how quickly the evolution of social media has occurred: MySpace is now only a footnote in the history of social media platforms.

Similarly, young people in the latter part of the 2010s began abandoning Facebook as their parents flooded the site. It was no longer cool to be on a platform where your mother could "friend" you. Though Facebook still has a hefty share of young users, more youth-oriented sites such as TikTok and Instagram (owned by Facebook, now Meta), have assumed dominance in the teenage space. One can only guess what the social media future will hold, but it is certain that budding Mark Zuckerbergs (co-founder of Facebook) and Jack Dorseys (co-founder of Twitter) are at work on it right now.

Social media use by teens has its detractors as well as its champions. This is no new phenomenon. Every new pastime adopted by teenagers has seen its share of criticism. In the 1930s and 40s, adults wondered aloud about the deleterious effects of violence in radio programming. The same concerns were voiced a couple of decades later when television assumed prominence. Comic books, too, have been viewed as corrupting the state of our youth. And later, of course, it was violence in video games that came under attack. So, the uproar about cyberbullying, and lack of privacy, and catfishing, and stalking, and other evils on social media is to be expected. Since social media has taken over the world in a way that none of its media predecessors, even television, could do, fears have been bound to follow.

This is not to say that social media is innocuous. Certainly, social media use has its downside, and teenagers and their parents would be foolish to completely ignore them. But, as with all media, we tend to focus on the very most negative or shocking stories. People have always loved to hear about the unordinary. One of MTV's rare successes in recent years is the reality show *Catfish*, which focuses on just one particular danger of social media. A catfish creates fake personal profiles on social media sites using someone else's pictures and false biographical information. This person then pretends to be someone else in an attempt to get an unsuspecting user to fall in love with them. Catfish may make up a tiny percentage of online users, but MTV seems to have found an unending array of them, as the show has been airing since 2012. And catfishing is not just a television phenomenon. Even a famous Notre Dame football player, Manti Te'o, fell victim to a sophisticated internet catfishing scheme and was devastated to learn that the young woman he was interacting with for years never existed.

Youth suicide is another shocking subject that is often raised as a potential evil of social media. Truly tragic stories of youths who have taken their lives make headlines. In some instances, lonely and depressed teens have been goaded by the malevolence of others into taking their own lives. Though statistics of youth social media suicides are minuscule, like catfishing, the danger is still out there, and teens and their parents must be discerning about whom they let into their lives. But the question remains as to whether such scenarios are actually caused by social media, or if social media merely provided a platform to create the inevitable. Victims' families have, on occasion, attempted to place blame on Facebook or other sites, but proving that social media is the culprit is a tall order in a court of law.

Compromised privacy is yet another danger of today's social media. More than ever, corporations are tracking what users do online. And why not? The use, distribution, and sale of customer data is a multibillion dollar phenomenon. Advertisers and marketers all want to be able to target their audiences so that their pitches are directed to the appropriate audience, and therefore, more likely to result in a sale. It is no accident that when someone searches for, say, a Nintendo Switch in Google, an ad for that video console appears in their Facebook feed 10 minutes later. When multibillionaire Facebook owner Mark Zuckerberg appeared before a somewhat hostile Congress in 2018, one of his questioners asked him how on earth Facebook made so much money when the service was free. "We sell ads, Senator," Zuckerberg responded. Viewers could almost hear him silently adding, "Duh."

No matter how much users believe that Facebook and its ilk are free, as the old saying goes, there is no free lunch. Customers pay by ceding their data—their likes, hobbies, education, work history, and more—to a corporation that knows just how to maximize profits by using that data. Teens (and their parents as well) aid Facebook by inputting all of this data themselves. And while Facebook and other social media corporations all make privacy options available, these companies still have all the data. And once the data is up there, it's fair game. Facebook users who have tried to quit the platform know that it is notoriously hard to completely erase a profile. Someday, in the not too far-off future, there will be millions of profiles of dead former social media users floating around in cyberspace. Teen users of Instagram would do well to consider seriously just how much of their lives they want to share with Mark Zuckerberg.

Opposing Viewpoints: Teens and Social Media presents a wide range of viewpoints that clarify and debate many of the above-mentioned issues. In chapters titled "Is Social Media Detrimental to the Mental Health of Teens?" "Who Should Bear Responsibility for Monitoring Teen Social Media Use?" "Is Cyberbullying of Teenagers a Serious Problem?" and "Is Teen Privacy at Risk on Social Media?", viewpoint authors debate the joys and hazards of navigating social media as a teen today, providing a valuable resource for those readers who want to investigate the multi-faceted world of teen social media use.

Notes

1. "Does Social Media Make Teens Unhappy? It May Depend on Their Age," by Virginia Hughes, *New York Times*, March 28, 2022.

Opposing Viewpoints® Series

Chapter 1

Is Social Media Detrimental to the Mental Health of Teens?

Chapter Preface

As they vie for eyeballs and clicks, many 21st-century media outlets have leaned in to more and more sensationalist stories. Negative and shocking pieces typically attract more viewers, and so, when it comes to social media and teen mental health, headlines such as these draw in fearful readers: "Is Social Media Threatening Teens' Mental Health and Well-being?"; "Does Social Media Make Teens Unhappy?"; and "How Social Media's Toxic Content Sends Teens into 'A Dangerous Spiral.'" These headlines do not come from scandal rags such as *The National Enquirer* and Breitbart News, but from esteemed sources such as *The New York Times* and Harvard University. When Pew Research Center reports that 24 percent of teens believe social media has a generally negative effect, the media tends to focus on the threat to mental health and ignore the 76 percent who did not agree with that statement. This is not to say that social media cannot be a treacherous place, only that there are many teens who have positive and enriching experiences online. As Virginia Hughes writes in *The New York Times*, "While a few researchers have claimed that digital technology is a powerful, causal factor in the rising rates of mental health problems, others have countered that the risk of harm for most teenagers is tiny—about the equivalent influence on well-being as wearing eyeglasses or regularly eating potatoes, one group calculated."

All of social media is a potential minefield, but there are sites where a teen may be less exposed to the threat of outright abuse, stalking, and bullying. The social media site Reddit, which bills itself as "the front page of the internet," can be worthwhile if teens are guided by their parents and avoid the topics deemed "nsfw," not safe for work. Reddit consists of thousands of subreddits on any and all possible subjects, hobbies, interests, etc. The posts in these subreddits are moderated by volunteers who have access to control the content within. The best moderators look out for the wellbeing of their members as well as the content. This is not to say that disagreements and a minor flare-up between users does not occur. But Reddit has one advantage over other social media: its users are anonymous, often going by clever and quirky user names that protect their privacy. Reddit also contains subreddits such as r/teenagers with content aimed at young people, though a caveat is in order here: due to the aforementioned anonymity of users, virtually anyone can post about anything on the subreddit.

Another social media platform that offers more control than some is Discord. The site comprised numerous "servers," which is their word for chatrooms, and, again, these spaces are moderated. Discord began as a site dedicated to gaming but has since expanded to include other interests. So, along with servers dedicated to Minecraft and Fortnite, one can also find groups that cater to the LGBT community, to metalheads, and to the National Football League. As Mollie Turner, who moderates a Discord server that was founded on a common interest in Japanese anime, says:

> As a social platform, Discord sets itself apart from others by fostering a true sense of community. Because groups intentionally gather based on interests, users can bond with others without feeling exposed to people actively looking to argue the merit of specific interests or "troll," and the moderation features allow for communities to maintain a sense of order. Plus, because anyone can create a server, there are endless opportunities for new communities to form.

Perhaps the number one takeaway teens can glean from social media regarding their mental health is that social media, like the internet in general, is what a user makes of it. The internet is essentially the world online. In any large group of people, there are those who are best avoided, whether in person or in the digital world. The viewpoints in this chapter cover a wide range of teen mental health issues, both negative and positive, in an attempt to provide a well-rounded tour of the topic.

Viewpoint 1

> *"Approximately 63% of teenagers report using social media every day. Additionally, 45% said they were on the internet 'almost constantly.' "*

Social Media Can Enhance Teens' Wellbeing When Used Properly

Taylor Christie

In the following viewpoint Taylor Christie argues that, with proper education and supervision, teens can use social media without negatively impacting their health or safety. Teenagers need to be socially connected, and social media can provide that connection. Using social media can have many valuable effects for teens. They can broaden their connections and understanding of the world; develop stronger communication and technical skills; enhance mental health and wellbeing; and develop meaningful relationships, among other positive outcomes. Yet social media can also impact teen wellbeing in negative ways. It is here that parents can help teens to navigate the pitfalls of social media. Taylor Christie is a marketing specialist and freelance writer.

As you read, consider the following questions:

1. What are some of the negative effects of social media on teens?
2. How can parents help teenagers deal with social media?

"How Does Social Media Affect Teenagers?" by Taylor Christie, Emplifi, April 24, 2020. Reprinted by permission.

3. How, according to the author, is learning about social media similar to learning to drive?

It's no secret that teenagers love their social media. Whether it's sharing photos on Instagram or performing a clever dance on TikTok, social media gives teens a sense of identity and belonging.

In fact, social media has become an essential part of everyday life for many teenagers between the ages of 13 and 17.

According to a recent study conducted by Pew Research Center, approximately 63% of teenagers report using social media every day. Additionally, 45% said they were on the internet "almost constantly."

Although these statistics may set off alarm bells for many parents, high social media usage doesn't have to be bad news. In fact, social media is often a place of collaborative learning, meaningful connections, and a support system for those who would otherwise experience exclusion.

With the proper instruction and supervision, teenagers can use social media as a valuable tool without jeopardizing their health or safety.

The Positive Effects of Social Media on Teenagers

Despite popular controversy, a crucial part of teenagers' psychological development is reliant on the ability to stay socially connected. Social media platforms such as Instagram, Facebook, and Twitter often provide young people with a unique online environment to chat with friends and stay updated on news.

In fact, social media has the potential to provide teenagers with valuable opportunities to develop skills and build a positive digital footprint. Here are five ways social media can make a positive impact:

Broaden Connections and Understanding of the World

Social media allows teenagers to appreciate different perspectives and worldviews to better understand the world we live in. With so much content shared across several different platforms, teenage users are given an opportunity to build a deeper knowledge on a variety of topics that interest them.

Moreover, social media encourages collaborative learning through exposing teens to current events, new ideas, and societal issues. In fact, social media drives teenagers to strengthen their real world skills and strengthen a sense of independence by exposing users to content outside of their immediate environment.

Develop Stronger Communication and Technical Skills

As the world becomes increasingly digitized, social media is now a part of everyday life. Learning how to effectively communicate online is a valuable skill to prepare teens for future work opportunities.

Additionally, teenagers with strong digital media literacy have a greater understanding of the role media plays in our society and how certain images or words may influence viewers. This may assist teens in recognizing fake news and question suspicious sources.

Provide Support for Mental Health and Wellbeing

The teenage years can be some of the most challenging as adolescents make the awkward transition to young adulthood. Fortunately, many social platforms often function as a place of support for those providing or seeking help during tough times.

Online support networks are especially important for teenagers as many students feel uncomfortable talking to close friends and family members about isolating issues such as sexual orientation, depression, or bullying. Oftentimes, online support groups are one of the few options available for struggling teens.

Remove Boundaries and Develop Meaningful Relationships

Unlike many other circumstances, social media allows teens the unique opportunity to connect with others who share similar ideas and interests. Teenagers have the ability to build friendships without the conventional restraints of geographical location or the burden of meeting and maintaining a relationship.

This feature is particularly useful for disabled children or those who may not feel accepted by their community. Additionally, teens may benefit from staying in closer contact with extended friends or family via networking on social media.

Build a Positive Digital Footprint

Social media platforms, such as LinkedIn or Handshake, allow users to share their accomplishments and showcase their talent to a professional network. Building a positive online portfolio is something teens can use to their advantage when applying to college or seeking employment.

Being active on a professional network also encourages teenagers to seek out valuable mentorship, as well as connect with career-driven groups.

Statistics on Social Media and Teen Mental Health

The activity of young people on social media largely mirrors their lives in the physical world: children and teenagers navigate the streams of their social networks, establishing new relationships, strengthening existing ones, and sometimes minimizing or ending them. Whether online or in the real world, young people will encounter bad behavior, whether it's directed at them or at someone or something else. How they respond to the bad behavior is an opportunity for them to learn important life skills.

The Pew Research Center's 2018 survey of U.S. teens determined that one in six teenagers have experienced at least one of six different forms of abusive behavior online:

- Name-calling (42%)
- Spreading false rumors (32%)
- Receiving unsolicited explicit images (25%)

The Potential Risks of Social Media

Although there are a number of developmental advantages, teenagers using social media should not go without concern. These are a few of the potential negative effects of social media on teenagers:

Disruption of Sleep and Focus

One of the most common problems that teenagers experience is a disruption in sleep patterns due to an excess consumption of social media. A University of Glasgow study found that the more adolescents used social media, the more likely they were to fall asleep later and wake up more often during the night.

Just like adults, teenagers often suffer from insomnia due to blue light emitted from smartphones. This ultimately leads to a

- Having their activities and whereabouts tracked by someone other than a parent (21%)
- Someone making physical threats (16%)
- Having explicit images of them shared without their consent (7%)

The survey found that 90% of teens believe online harassment is a problem for people their age, and 63% identify it as a "major problem." Yet, the most recent Pew survey of teenagers' use of social media and other technology, also conducted in 2018, revealed some interesting findings. It found that only 24% of teens believe social media has a generally negative effect, while 31% say its effect is positive and 45% believe its impact is neither positive nor negative.

The teens who think social media is generally a negative influence say it increases bullying and rumor-mongering (27%), or it harms relationships and makes them less meaningful (17%). However, only a small number believe social media use could "lead to psychological issues or drama."

"Impact of Social Media on Youth Mental Health: Statistics, Tips & Resources," The University of Nevada, Reno.

chronic lack of sleep, eventually affecting attention span and the ability to focus.

Luckily, there is a quick and simple solution to this seemingly impossible issue. According to SCL Health, electronic devices should be shut off at least 30 minutes before bed to eliminate blue light emissions and activate the natural circadian rhythm.

Developing Unrealistic Views and Peer Pressure

Even as adults, we all have a tendency to compare ourselves to the picture perfect model seen on the screen. However, teenagers are nearly twice as likely to subject themselves to harmful comparisons.

According to a study from the University of Kentucky, adolescents are especially vulnerable because they are undergoing a lot of physical, social, and psychological changes.

Parents and mentors should be proactive in strengthening their teens digital literacy skills in order to avoid feelings of diminished self-esteem or negative body image. Monitoring content and establishing open dialogue about setting realistic expectations are constructive ways parents can prepare their teen for the responsibility of social media.

Loss of Privacy and Diminished Security

Unfortunately, the internet is not always a safe place for naive or inexperienced users. Whether it's oversharing private details online or chatting with strangers, teenagers are far more likely to be the victim of harassment.

In order to avoid the potential dangers of social media, teenagers should always keep their accounts private and lookout for the facade many online predators use. Parents can play a key role in keeping their teen safe by educating them about online privacy.

Finding the Perfect Balance

There are several things parents can do to allow their teens to enjoy the many benefits of social media without compromising their mental or physical health. It's important to curate rules and boundaries together in order to preserve your teen's autonomy while safeguarding them from risks.

Parents play a crucial role in how social media affects teenagers, and the positive boundaries they can setup often look like this:

- Establish reasonable time limits that incorporate a digital curfew
- Monitor your teens account on a regular basis to ensure they are using it responsibly
- Communicate expectations about what's acceptable and unacceptable behavior on social media
- Encourage face-to-face social interaction to avoid heightened anxiety or digital dependency
- Set a positive example by sharing your own healthy social media habits

A great way to further understand your child's interests and perspective on social media is to get to know the popular platforms. Read more about what teens are looking for on social media platforms by checking out brands that rule on TikTok or ways to stand out on Instagram.

The Takeaway

Ultimately, social media education is just like learning how to drive. Newbies will need more support and direction as they develop their digital literacy skills and learn how to navigate social media.

Over time, teens should have the opportunity to build trust through demonstrating responsible digital behavior. Although social media poses obvious risks, it's a part of everyday life and a powerful tool for teens who know how to use it responsibly.

Viewpoint 2

> *"Thirty-two percent of teen girls said that when they felt bad about their bodies, Instagram made them feel worse."*

Highly Visual Social Media Has a Negative Effect on Teens

Molly Callahan

In the following viewpoint, Molly Callahan interviews Northeastern University Professor Rachel Rodgers about the negative effects that highly visual social media platforms can have on young teenagers. Acknowledging that the teenage years are a highly vulnerable period, Rodgers suggests that the visual nature of apps such as Instagram can lead teens to feel inferior about their bodies when confronted by more perfect images on social media. But it is difficult for teenagers to steer their social media preferences in healthy, positive directions, given that the algorithms on these platforms often do the opposite, by presenting teens with images that intimidate teens. Social media has a responsibility to these teens to provide a safe and healthy environment. Molly Callahan is a senior reporter for News@Northeastern at Northeastern University.

"Why Does Instagram Have a Negative Effect on Teenagers' Mental Health?" by Molly Callahan, News@Northeastern, Northeastern University, September 20, 2021. Reprinted by permission.

As you read, consider the following questions:

1. According to Rachel Rodgers, how is a teenager a bit like an animal whose shells are still growing to protect them?
2. How is the experience of viewing images on social media different from consuming visuals in more traditional formats such as magazines?
3. What advice does Rodgers offer about navigating social media in healthy, positive ways?

Since at least March 2020, Facebook officials have known that Instagram—the photo-sharing app owned by Facebook, Inc.—has the power to make teenagers feel worse about their bodies, according to an internal report obtained by *The Wall Street Journal*.

"Thirty-two percent of teen girls said that when they felt bad about their bodies, Instagram made them feel worse," Facebook researchers wrote in the presentation about the negative effects of Instagram, according to the Journal.

The effect may have as much to do with the mechanics of the app itself as with its audience, says Rachel Rodgers, associate professor of applied psychology at Northeastern. The highly visual nature of social media platforms favored by younger people—TikTok, Snapchat, and Instagram—put a social premium on appearance, says Rodgers, who studies sociocultural influences on body image and eating concerns. At the same time, the adolescents drawn to them are still developing their sense of identity.

"It's a bit like animals whose shells are still growing to protect them; it's a really vulnerable time," she says.

But, Rodgers says, there is a way to engage with these social platforms in a more balanced, healthier way. It just takes a lot of work.

What did you make of the findings about the negative effects of Instagram obtained by *The Wall Street Journal*?

I can't comment on what Facebook may have collected in terms of their own data or how they went about that, but I think substantively around the question of whether or not these and other platforms are related to negative mental health impacts—particularly among young people—we know from a lot of independent research that that has been shown to be the case.

Particularly in the areas I'm most familiar with, we know there are effects on young people's feelings about their appearance, their body satisfaction, and social media platforms can increase risk for eating disorders and other mental health concerns such as depression and low self-esteem. We know that cyberbullying occurs among young people, we know that for some young people, the consequences of that can be extremely damaging. There's no doubt that there's substantial research showing that these platforms can have a negative effect on young people.

What is it about using these types of social media apps that has such an effect on mental health?

There's a conjunction between what it is about the application and what it is about the audience.

In my opinion, which is supported by data, there are a lot of things that make the apps deleterious: There's the fact that the more popular applications with young folks are highly visual. You're only consuming pictures and you're also invited to only produce pictures of yourself. Both of those things orient you towards thinking that your appearance is a really important piece of you—if you're only seeing photos of other people and only posting photos of yourself, it emphasizes that appearance is a really important part of self-worth, which we know is a risky way of considering appearance because intrinsically appearance is going to change over time.

These apps are also highly interactive—one of the points of posting is to get feedback. Obviously, you always hope that feedback is going to be positive, but every young person knows that that's not always the case, either because they themselves have gotten negative feedback or because they've witnessed someone receiving negative feedback. In a conceptualization where you are only worth what your picture is, that's a direct reflection of your worth as a person. So, that becomes very impactful.

And then there's the fact that there's a real blurring between corporate interests and individual interests.

Then, you bring those characteristics together with younger people who are developing their identity. As an older adult, there are a number of things in your life that you can achieve that can put appearance in the background or balance out a negative experience, but when you're 14, you don't have that. It's a bit like animals whose shells are still growing to protect them; it's a really vulnerable time.

How is the experience of viewing images on Instagram, Snapchat, or TikTok different from consuming them in magazines?

Teens are still developing an understanding of marketing intent and the amount of affection and curation that goes into images in any kind of post, really. The level of literacy around the fact that these images are highly curated and often digitally altered is really variable. You hear people say, "Well this is a video on TikTok, so it must be real because you can't alter videos." And of course, you can filter videos just like you can filter photos. There's a disconnect around the likelihood that this was edited in some way and how "real" is it?

But there's also some difficulty in understanding that even if this post isn't explicitly selling me a product, it was placed here with a particular self-promoting intent. Nobody posts to social media in the hopes that people think they're unattractive, unpopular, someone you wouldn't want to hang out with.

There's also the added wrinkle of algorithms that can fill your feed with ads based on what they think you're interested in—how does that play a role?

If we're thinking about adolescence and the importance of norms: If you think that what you're seeing is the same as what everybody else is seeing, that peer pressure is going to make a much stronger impact on you than, say, somebody who's 25 years old.

Is there a way to engage with these apps as a younger person that will be healthier or more balanced?

I think there is, and I think there are intrinsic limitations to these apps.

Some of the difficulties that are software-related are how hard it is to tell the algorithms you don't like something. You can try to play them by overexposing them to the things you do want to see, and that will kind of automatically reduce the things you don't. But Facebook and Instagram don't have dislike functions, it's really hard to say "I don't like this, I don't want to see it."

The other thing is that they're highly visual—it's really hard to interact on Snapchat or Instagram that doesn't somehow talk about appearance because text just isn't a big part of it.

I do think that young people can interact with these in better ways and some of them really do, but when they describe that, you see how effortful it is and how deliberate it has to be and the way that it, in some ways, sort of sets them apart. You can spend a lot of time getting the algorithms to learn the type of things you're interested in and then they will show you prosocial content [content that encourages prosocial behavior, or behavior through which people benefit others] or the brands that are high on corporate responsibility or sustainability or whatever your values may be.

You can also be very deliberate about who you follow, what you follow, to try to curate your online space. You can be careful about how much time you spend on it. You can choose not to participate in the pressure to make yourself highly visible, but again this is onerous as a young person because it means asking people not to tag you, and explaining that you don't have one when people ask for your handle.

I do think it's somewhat telling that the best way to do this healthfully is just not to do it.

Do these companies have a responsibility to the young people who are using their platforms to make it easier to use them in a healthy way?

I would personally say that we all as humans have a responsibility to make the world a safe, equitable, prosocial place. I would agree that companies do, and I think that's true of all companies: It's true for clothing companies and beauty companies, all companies that profit from making people feel that their appearance is inadequate. I think it's also true of us and other users. It's a social responsibility, it's something that the people who are deriving the most benefit from should care the most about.

Viewpoint 3

> *"Encouragingly, the young people we spoke to were also highly critical users of social media and thought carefully about the content they were engaging with online. For instance, the teenagers reported that they would often ignore content that had the potential to lead to harm...."*

Many Teens Are Savvy About Social Media Use

Victoria Goodyear and Mikael Quennerstedt

In the following viewpoint, Victoria Goodyear and Mikael Quennerstedt report findings that are at odds with the common concern that social media is unhealthy for teens. A research study found that teens can use social media to enhance their lives and that many teens tend to be discriminating about what they will read and view online. Many teens have developed coping mechanisms to deal with the reality that their bodies may not measure up to social media's images of perfection. And while social media can expose teens' vulnerability, it can also greatly enhance their quality of life. Victoria Goodyear is Senior Lecturer in Pedagogy in Sport Physical Activity and Health at the University of Birmingham's School of Sport, Exercise and Rehabilitation Sciences in Birmingham, England. Mikael Quennerstedt is Professor in Physical Education and Health at Örebro University, Sweden.

As you read, consider the following questions:

1. How do many teens deal with inappropriate content online, according to the authors?
2. How do some teens use irony to deal with pictures they post online that may not measure up to social media's images of perfection?
3. How can social media expose teens' vulnerabilities?

We often hear of the harms of social media on teens and young people, especially on their mental health and self-esteem. And while it's true that there is evidence of links between the two, our latest research on young girls and young boys has revealed that social media isn't always negative for young people.

In some cases, we found, it can actually positively influence their health and wellbeing, by helping them learn about healthy eating, or about new workouts to try. We also found that social media provided a space for young people to talk to each other about issues of health.

For our study, conducted by researchers from the University of Birmingham and Örebro University, we recruited over 1,300 young girls and boys, aged 13-18, from ten UK schools. We were interested in better understanding how young people use social media, and how they feel it impacts their health and wellbeing.

To do this we selected 84 participants from the main sample and had them take part in small focus group interviews. The teenagers shared examples of health-related social media posts that they had accessed or used (such as smoothie recipes, a workout, or a celebrity's post), and then explained why and how they had used the information in the social media post.

They also discussed the types of social media posts they would ignore and not use (such as workouts that were not age appropriate). They were then asked about how they used social media as part of their daily lives and how they thought it affected their health and wellbeing.

The results showed that social media often had a positive influence on the young people's motivation to be physically active and on their ability to make conscious diet choices. Social media also allowed them to access information they found inspirational, and learn about different apps they could use to be physically active or monitor their progress. They reported that likes, comments, and views on their social media posts also helped them stay motivated to exercise.

Encouragingly, the young people we spoke to were also highly critical users of social media and thought carefully about the content they were engaging with online. For instance, the teenagers reported that they would often ignore content that had the potential to lead to harm, such as images or videos that presented unrealistic workouts or expectations for their bodies.

A Longitudinal Study

Long-term use of social media websites did not negatively affect mental health, according to an 8-year longitudinal study published in Computers in Human Behavior.

The study recruited 500 participants (51.6% girls) from an ongoing, longitudinal study of inner family life involving families with children aged between 10 years and 13 years.

Participants responded during each of the eight waves regarding how many hours they spent per day using social networking sites like Facebook, Instagram and others. Responses varied from 1 hour to more than 8 hours per day. Depression in adolescents was evaluated using the 20-item, self-reported Center for Epidemiological Studies Depression Scale for Children with responses ranging from low to high feelings of depression. Anxiety was measured using the six-item generalized anxiety disorder subscale from the Spence Child Anxiety Inventory where results raged from no feelings of anxiety to always feeling anxiety.

#Gymlads vs #SkinnyGirls

Our study also showed that boys and girls interacted with social media differently, revealing different, gendered, concerns about health and wellbeing.

Boys tended to report accessing health-related information to help them be more physically active and used social media to chat with friends. But many said they experienced pressure from social media to look "ripped" (muscular) but not too slim.

To cope with this pressure, many told us that they used irony and humour in their posts to avoid ridicule from friends, or as a coping mechanism if they felt they didn't "fit in" because of their physique. For instance, the boys in our study explained how they used the hashtag #gymlad when posting selfies. While some used it in a literal sense (if their body was ripped), others used it ironically.

Our results indicate that girls, on the other hand, tend to use social media apps like Snapchat and Instagram to learn about

> Data showed that social media use did not seem to be a significant risk factor for development in depression and anxiety. In the 8-year study, no associations between time spent on social media and the outcome of participants' mental health were recorded.
>
> The investigators wrote that future research should examine the context and content centered around social media and consider other factors that might offer an explanation in the increase in mental health issues during adolescence and emerging adulthood. This future research could gain a more clinically based and professional way of assessing mental health and could examine lifetime impacts of social media use.
>
> "If they increased their social media time, would it make them more depressed? Also, if they decreased their social media time, were they less depressed? The answer is no. We found that time spent on social media was not what was impacting anxiety or depression."
>
> **"Mental Health Not Impacted by Long-Term Social Media Use," Healio, November 8, 2019.**

health, and to find support from friends and followers and keep in touch with their peers.

But the girls also said that they were wary of skinny or fat shaming online, and were on constant alert of such posts. Many also said they faced contradictory pressures to be thin but not too thin, and that while it was acceptable to be "fake" (for example, through the use of filters on their photos), many felt that they couldn't be "too fake", and that a natural look was preferred. To avoid being skinny or fat shamed, many told us they used terms like "chunky monkey" in their posts—even if they knew they were thin.

Although many of the young people's experiences of social media were positive in terms of health, it was evident that some of the time, they found themselves in a position of vulnerability. Some said they experienced bullying and heightened levels of body dysmorphia on social media. We found that these risks were particularly evident when their online profiles were public, and when the content shared by others, including their friends, made them feel bad about their bodies. If young people are vulnerable, for whatever reason, social media use has the potential to intensify those vulnerabilities.

While the risks should certainly not be overlooked, our findings show that social media can actually be positive for young people's health and wellbeing. We also know from other research that a benefit of social media is that it provides real-time, low-cost information, and support from peers. Empowering young people to use social media safely, critically and responsibly may thus help them continue to live healthy lives.

Viewpoint 4

> *"Social media can be a total waste of time or a platform that changes the world."*

Many Teens Benefit from Social Media

Parven Kaur

In the following viewpoint, Parven Kaur examines the positive side of social media, which she claims, is often overlooked by those who focus only on negatives. Kaur cites the examples of young entrepreneurs who have started businesses through their use of social media. Whether social media platforms are good or bad is in the eye of the beholder, Kaur claims. It is important for parents to monitor their children's social media use and steer them in the proper direction. Parven Kaur is the founder of Kids N Clicks, a web resource that help parents and children thrive in a digital world. She has extensive experience in the digital and social media arena and has been a consultant for various charitable organizations across Scotland.

As you read, consider the following questions:

1. What are some of the benefits of social media use, according to the author?
2. What are some examples of young people who have started businesses through social media?
3. How can parents motivate their children to use social media in positive ways?

"Benefits of Social Media for Tweens and Teens," by Parven Kaur, Kids N Clicks, April 27, 2020. Reprinted by permission.

The benefits of social media are rarely discussed. Reading online we may stumble hundreds of articles about the negative impact of social media, but not the benefits of it.

Now that children are stuck at home, we find ourselves connecting with others through social media. The same also goes for children.

But beyond connection, there are plenty of benefits of social media for youth. For instance, building a business, finding a job, showcasing talent, and many more.

Now let's go through how your children can benefit from being on social media and use it productively.

Benefits of Social Media for Tweens and Teens:

1. To start a business
2. Showcase a talent
3. Learn new things
4. Share kindness
5. Form study groups
6. Strengthen mental health
7. Feel connected
8. Build technical skills
9. Create positive digital footprint

Let's go through each one of those benefits in more detail.

#1 Benefits of Social Media: Start a Business

This is one of the biggest advantages of social media but rarely thought about by parents.

It is becoming more common for parents to think of business for kids that can teach them the value of money from a young age.

Online business and social media are becoming the most common way to start a business.

There are plenty of young adults who started a business through social media.

Parents are always worried that their teenagers may be spending too much time on their devices.

But is spending time on social media really that bad for a teenager? It all depends on how your child uses it.

Social media can be a total waste of time or a platform that changes the world.

We hear a lot of young people turning into millionaires at a very young age.

This is something more common among Gen Z (16–22 years old).

Many of this is driven by social media and their ability to turn friends into customers.

While many teenagers spend time on social media for entertainment purposes there is a group of teenagers that seeks business opportunities on those platforms.

Now let's check out these teen bosses.

Successful Kids Doing Business on Social Media

1. Rosie Ackland, 21-year-old founded Beach Knickers.

Beach Knickers is a vintage clothing brand that sells beachwear as well as nighties.

She got an inspiration to create this brand when she spotted a gap in the market. Rosie said that all the beachwear she found on the high street was skimpy and she just wanted something cute.

She uses Facebook and Instagram to connect with customers.

2. Annelise Katz, founded Nails on Cornwall

She uses Instagram to promote her gel manicure company. Instagram has enabled her to promote her business by posting images of her manicures.

She encourages her customers to post pictures of their completed her nails and tag her on it.

3. Jake Miller, 21-years old founded Unfiltered

Unfiltered is a company that interviews important business leaders all around the world.

Jake now has over 200 video interviews with business leaders such as Richard Branson, Ian Wright, Sam Altman and many more. In an interview with Forbes magazine Jake says that social media played an important role in making his business a success.

He finds the right target audience using Facebook Sponsored ads and Instagram ads.

#2 Benefits of Social Media: Showcase a Talent

Many youth are turning to YouTube and TikTok to showcase their talent.

Your child could be a good singer, artist, or anyone with a special talent to show to the world. There is no better way then to put it out on social media.

Believe it or not, Justin Bieber was discovered through YouTube.

He was discovered in 2001 [by] his manager by accident when searching for a different artist. The rest is history.

Your child might not be the next Justin Bieber but you never know where his talent can take him/her when it is shared with the world.

#3 Benefits of Social Media: Learn New Things

How many times have we turned to YouTube to learn something new? The same goes for our kids. This is one of the biggest benefits of social media

When they are watching a YouTube video, it could be that they are trying to learn something new.

There's plenty of kids teaching school subjects on YouTube. You can encourage your children to learn new things on social media.

It does not have to be educational, it could be something fun like learning how to create the new viral TikTok videos.

Whatever reason they choose to be on YouTube or any other social media platform, there are plenty of learning opportunities for them.

Social media can also positively impact your kid's interest in a certain subject. For example, looking at cooking videos your child might be interested to learn how to cook.

#4 Benefits of Social Media: Share Kindness

Social media can be a great place for children to share kindness with others.

You might not remember or know about the story of a boy who was bullied because of his homemade T-shirt design.

The fourth-grader made his own University of Tennessee T-shirt for College Colors Day. Other kids started making fun of him

The teacher then posted on social media how disappointed she was by the way this boy was being treated. Her post went viral.

Outpouring love and support was given to this boy. His T-shirt design is now sold online.

#5 Benefits of Social Media: Feel Connected

Now more than ever we are relying on social media to keep in touch with our friends.

Social media can be a very powerful tool for children to stay connected with their friends.

Plenty of apps, like Facebook, Instagram and TikTok have been a source of connection for teens.

#6 Benefits of Social Media: Form Study Groups

Facebook groups have been popular for children to study together. Kids share their homework, discuss assignments, and post things relevant to schoolwork.

Using Facebook group your child can also organize Live chats about homework.

This is particularly useful when a child is absent from school but can get information from friends who are in school that day.

Many students use Facebook group to share notes with other students.

#7 Benefits of Social Media: Strengthen Mental Health

All this while we have been reading about the negative effects of social media on our mental health. For example, cyberbullying, and more.

But social media has also been a place for support for young people.

For children with disability social media makes them feel connected for others in the community.

Typing a certain hashtag, for example, #loneliness on Instagram will result in hundreds of accounts to provide support for those going through a difficult time.

Social media can be a great place for young people who feel like they cannot talk about their problems with anyone else.

#8 Benefits of Social Media: Build a Positive Digital Footprint

Your social media account can act like your CV. There is no doubt that employers and college administrators will go through an applicant's social media account.

This is a great place to build that positive impact and create a positive online portfolio.

#9 Benefits of Social Media: Build Technical Skills

Social media is now just part of a child's life growing up. It is important to have the right skills when communicating online.

This will help children prepare for future jobs. Social media gives them a good platform to practice online communicating skills by interacting with friends and family.

This Is How We Can Motivate Teenagers to Utilize Social Media in a Positive Manner

1. Have an Open Conversation

Parents tend to head towards the negative mindset when they see their teenager spending hours on their mobile devices.

Instead of assuming the worst, it is important to gain an understanding of what your teen is utilizing those platforms for.

Speak to your teenager what he/she uses social media for.

If you are aware that your teenager is a blogger, vlogger or YouTuber then do encourage them to keep working hard towards their goals.

Do not discourage them by telling them to get a "real" job. The future is digital and building your name in the online world is competitive and involves a lot of hard work.

If you know for sure your teenager is not using those platforms for a positive reason then speak to them about what other teenagers are doing online.

This might encourage them to do something good for themselves.

2. Identify Business Opportunities on Social Media

There are always 2 ways to look at a coin. Rather than looking at social media as a place to have fun, get them to start thinking of it as a place to start a business.

You can support them by saying that you are willing to pay for a sponsored Facebook ad on a particular budget if they can spot a gap in the market.

If you know your teenager has a particular talent or interest in a subject matter then encourage them to share it on social media.

For instance, if your teenager has a hobby in painting then encourage him/her to sell it on platforms such as Etsy.

If your child is passionate about maths or any subject then encourage them to start a YouTube video.

The beauty of building a business online will give your teen the flexibility to work on the business at hours that is convenient to them. It does not have to come in between their school or college time. They can work on it on a part-time basis.

3. Follow the Right People on Social Media

There are some social media influencers that can have a positive influence on your teen.

Following influences such as Simon Sinek, Gary Vaynerchuk, and Mari Smith can encourage your teenager to go after their goals.

There are plenty of technical and life skills you can learn by following the right people. Social media can be a powerful learning tool.

You can learn so many business skills from your followers.

They have gone through the challenges of starting a business and can help you find a better solution. Encourage your teen to use their online time to learn income-generating techniques.

4. Set Time Limit and Restrictions

While social media can be beneficial, we can't ignore the dangers that come with it.

- Talk to your child about internet safety
- Make sure they are at least 13 years old before signing up on social media
- Set screen time limit

Conclusion

Parents need to understand that not all Gen Z are lazy, selfish, and self-conscious.

There are teens who are working hard and spending hours on social media to network and build relationships.

Many of them are using those platforms to achieve their goals. If your teen is one of them then do not discourage them rather nurture their interests or business goals.

Older generation parents need to start realising that the future is digital.

If you feel your teen is using those platforms only for entertainment purposes then have a conversation with them.

Speak to them about the potential they may have on those platforms and how you as a parent are willing to support them.

Viewpoint 5

> *"There are only two industries that call their customers 'users': illegal drugs and software."*

Heavy Social Media Use Is a Habit Some May Wish to Break

Ian A. Anderson and Wendy Wood

In the following viewpoint, Ian A. Anderson and Wendy Wood refute the popular belief that heavy social media use is always addictive. Unlike addiction, heavy users of social media may benefit, while others may suffer. They believe that a "habit" is a better way to describe the behavior of heavy users, rather than an "addiction." Social media companies benefit from such habits: heavy users are their bread and butter, according to the authors. Heavy users may want to break their habit, and the authors provide suggestions as to how they may do so. Ian A. Anderson is a Ph.D. Student at the USC Dornsife College of Letters, Arts and Sciences. Wendy Wood is Provost Professor of Psychology and Business, at the USC Dornsife College of Letters, Arts and Sciences.

"No, You Are Not Addicted to Your Digital Device, but You May Have a Habit You Want to Break," by Ian A. Anderson and Wendy Wood, The Conversation, February 2, 2021. https://theconversation.com/no-you-are-not-addicted-to-your-digital-device-but-you-may-have-a-habit-you-want-to-break-153860.

As you read, consider the following questions:

1. Why do the authors prefer the word "habit" to "addiction" to refer to those who spend a great deal of time on social media?
2. How does seeing heavy internet use as a habit provide a means for users to break free of their dependence on social media?
3. What are some specific suggestions the authors offer to help end excessive use of social media?

Imagine that you're a typical middle school student having dinner with your family. Your mother takes your smartphone away and puts it in a lock-box that won't open for an hour.

Would you: (a) go ahead and eat dinner with your family? (b) try to pry open the box? or (c) smash the box with a heavy tool when your family is sufficiently distracted?

As depicted in Netflix's popular documentary, "The Social Dilemma," the answer is first (b)—if that doesn't work, then (c). Apparently, for youth, being connected online is akin to an addictive substance: "There are only two industries that call their customers 'users': illegal drugs and software," as information design expert Edward Tufte has put it.

Popular media fuels this portrait, with testimonials from extreme users and highlights of their behavior. So-called addicts who changed their lives through digital detox confess that social media was killing them. The health care industry has capitalized on this digital detox trend, depicting extreme use as the norm. Scholars, too, debate ways to define and prevent addiction to digital media.

It's a mistake, however, to equate frequent social media use with addiction. Just the label carries stigma—a personal failing or pathology that has significant negative outcomes to the user and their family, such as lost jobs and destroyed relationships.

As researchers who study habits and social media use, we have found that excessive social media use can be a very strong habit. But that doesn't make it an addiction.

The Upside of Social Media

Unlike addiction, frequent social media users sometimes benefit and sometimes suffer. That's why a more accurate description is "habit."

Habits form naturally through repeated use. Use any site or app enough, and you'll form associations in memory between cues, such as site alerts and your smartphone, and responses, such as logging on. Once habits have formed, perception of cues automatically makes you think of logging on.

Creating user habits is central to the business of social media platforms like Facebook, TikTok and Twitter. Their revenue rises from high-frequency users. Lots of infrequent users either have no effect on revenue or are a drag on the bottom line. User habits are integral to the success and design of social media platforms.

Most of us start using social media because it is rewarding. The likes, follows and friends we accumulate are all rewards. Take Instagram: Almost 70% of user postings can be explained by a reward-learning model in which likes are analogous to the food pellets that teach rats to pull a lever in a Skinner box. Get enough likes on your posts, and you will start to post more often and create an Instagram posting habit.

How Platforms Design Around Habits

Social media platforms have figured out how to make pallid online rewards as real to humans as food pellets are to rats. Likes and followers gain fuel when they become public. Users then engage in social comparisons, feeling good when they gain social recognition and bad when others' accomplishments diminish their own. Social pressure is part of the experience.

Even more rewards come from the algorithms that curate our social media sites to appeal to our personal interests. This is the source of echo chambers, creating a cheering crowd for most everyone.

Habits also explain the design of successful platform features. Consider the endless scroll. It effectively removes points that might signal you to stop reading. Just as important, it presents each post in a sequence, which heightens your experience of rewards (amazing cat video!) interspersed with the ho-hum. Such intermittent rewards are especially effective at building habits.

Once habits have formed, recurring cues—like notifications and the usual places and times that we use the app—trigger social media use. If you repeatedly scroll your Twitter feed while riding the bus, for example, then you may find that your Twitter habit is activated merely by sitting down on the seat.

Habits function largely outside of our conscious awareness and your intentions. But once in a while, you come up against your habits and realize they are there. Frequent social media users might experience habits like this during a phishing attack. Frequent users should be most knowledgeable about security risks and how to avoid them, but acting habitually and responding without thinking made these users vulnerable to responding automatically to phishing attacks. These moments allow us to "see" our habits up close.

A More Empowering Narrative for Social Media Users

Habits also explain why the addiction model, though inaccurate, is pervasive. Habits keep people automatically using social media even when intending to do otherwise. When users find it hard to quit, they may feel addicted. Users adopt narratives validating feelings of addiction and share these widely. However, these narratives actually disempower users. They inhibit our understanding of how to stop or control social media use.

Understanding habits allows us to reverse engineer our way out of social media's behavioral traps. In other words, we can change the cues that activate our habits. Without those cues, habits are simply not activated. But cues that trigger habits are also their Achilles' heel.

Consider the findings from our analysis of more than 9,000 Facebook users. After a change in site design, those with strong habits immediately reduced their posting rates. The changes in platform cues appeared to disrupt habitual users. They didn't show the cravings you'd expect with addiction. They just used it less. In contrast, the design change—which was implemented to increase posting—did just that for occasional users.

You can take advantage of this Achilles' heel yourself. Try modifying or eliminating cues from your smartphone and apps, including turning the phone screen face down, putting it on airplane mode or turning off notifications.

It can also help to add friction so that you have to think before you log on. Students in a recent study were able to decrease social media use by simply putting their phone charger farther away or making their phone less accessible by putting it in their purse rather than pants pocket.

So, that hated lock-box for smartphones during family dinners might actually work.

By understanding habits, we all can stop worrying about digital detox and start reengineering apps and websites to meet our own needs as opposed to the sites' needs—which is to build a habitual user base. And we can get on with ameliorating the real challenges of social media: misinformation, biased algorithms and the disruptions they create.

Periodical and Internet Sources Bibliography

The following articles have been selected to supplement the diverse views presented in this chapter.

Cristina Criddle, "Social media damages teenagers' mental health, report says," BBC. January 27, 2022. https://www.bbc.com/news/technology-55826238.

Rachel Ehmke, "How Using Social Media Affects Teenagers," Child Mine Institute. https://childmind.org/article/how-using-social-media-affects-teenagers/.

Jasmine Glasheen, "Are Facebook and Instagram Toxic for Young Consumers?" Robin Report. October 5, 2021. https://www.therobinreport.com/are-facebook-and-instagram-toxic-for-young-consumers/.

Sherri Gordon, "5 Ways Social Media Affects Teen Mental Health," Verywell Family. November 7, 2021. https://www.verywellfamily.com/ways-social-media-affects-teen-mental-health-4144769.

Jonathan Haidt, "The Dangerous Experiment on Teen Girls," *Atlantic*. November 21, 2021. https://www.theatlantic.com/ideas/archive/2021/11/facebooks-dangerous-experiment-teen-girls/620767/.

Virginia Hughes, "Does Social Media Make Teens Unhappy? It May Depend on Their Age." *New York Times*. March 28, 2022. https://www.nytimes.com/2022/03/28/science/social-media-teens-mental-health.html.

Katie Hurley, "Social Media and Teens: How Does Social Media Affect Teenagers' Mental Health," Psycom. November 16, 2020. https://www.psycom.net/social-media-teen-mental-health.

Anya Kamenetz, "Facebook's own data is not as conclusive as you think about teens and mental health." NPR. October 6, 2021. https://www.npr.org/2021/10/06/1043138622/facebook-instagram-teens-mental-health.

Niall McCrae, "Think Social Media Is to Blame for Teens' Depression? Think Again," *Newsweek*. March 6, 2017. https://www.newsweek.com/twitter-depression-facebook-social-media-study-564228.

Elina Mir, Caroline Novas, and Meg Seymour, "Social Media and Adolescents' and Young Adults' Mental Health," The National Center for Health Research. https://www.center4research.org/social-media-affects-mental-health/.

Jacqueline Nesi, "The Impact of Social Media on Youth Mental Health: Challenges and Opportunities," *North Carolina Medical Journal.* March 2020, 81 (2) 116-121. https://www.ncmedicaljournal.com/content/81/2/116.

Benjamin Plackett, "Social Media is Having a Negative Impact on Teenagers' Mental Health," *Discover Magazine.* January 28, 2022. https://www.discovermagazine.com/mind/social-media-is-having-a-negative-impact-on-teenagers-mental-health.

Nicole Wetsman, "Social media might be bad for teens' mental health at certain age windows," The Verge. March 29, 2021. https://www.theverge.com/2022/3/29/23000460/social-media-mental-health-window-puberty.

Mary Elizabeth Williams, "Why teens are self-diagnosing on TikTok," Salon. April 9, 2022. https://www.salon.com/2022/04/09/why-teens-are-self-diagnosing-on-tiktok/.

OPPOSING VIEWPOINTS® SERIES

Chapter 2

Who Should Bear Responsibility for Monitoring Teen Social Media Use?

Chapter Preface

They call it the 26 words that created the internet. In the early days of the world wide web, when America Online (AOL) still provided the number one platform by which to access the internet, the U.S. Congress passed a law that has had a profound effect on online dialogue to this day. Seeking to promote free speech on the web at the same time as they wished to deter harmful and illegal language, Congress in 1996 agreed to support Section 230 of the Communications Decency Act. The 26 words that ensured the survival of the internet as we know it read:

> No provider or user of an interactive computer service shall be treated as the publisher or speaker of any information provided by another information content provider.

In other words, early internet providers such as AOL, Prodigy, and Compuserve could not be held liable for the content that users wrote on their sites. Section 230 also gave internet platforms the right, and the duty, to remove harmful or illegal content. But Congress in the mid-1990s could not have foreseen the meteoric rise of social media sites such as Facebook, Tik Tok, and Instagram. Social media companies seeking to eliminate harmful or illegal material were simply swamped by the sheer magnitude of posts. Today, there are literally billions of posts being shared on social media sites. Facebook users alone post half-a-million comments every minute! One can easily see how, even if social media companies had the best of intentions and were not primarily concerned with the bottom line (making money), monitoring and moderating such overwhelming amounts of data would be virtually impossible.

And that's how social media in the 21st century became the wild west.

Freedom of speech is a wonderful concept. But like all good things, it can be manipulated. Today, misinformation is about as common as information on social media. In Congress, Democrats and Republicans alike decry how social media has allowed speech that they do not approve of to spread like wildfire. They have now sought to hold social media companies more accountable, but how to do so without shutting down freedom of speech remains a dilemma.

Those in favor of holding social media companies accountable received an unexpected gift when, in 2021, Frances Haugen, a Harvard-educated data scientist at Facebook, turned whistleblower. She collected and subsequently released thousands of documents implicating Facebook in shady and corrupt activity. Haugen stated on the influential television news show *60 Minutes*, and later on, before Congress, that Facebook harms children, creates division, and undermines democracy in pursuit of breakneck growth and "astronomical profits." Haugen further alleged that Facebook was aware, through its own surveys and studies, of the harm it was doing, especially to young people. But the information was ignored in the pursuit of growth and money.

Such revelations, combined with flattening user growth, caused Facebook stock to plummet from a high of $380 per share to under $200. Young people are gravitating toward other platforms, such as Instagram, but there's a catch—Facebook owns Instagram!

Whether citizens and Congress will be able to hold social media accountable is uncertain. Already, since the Haugen revelations, some parents of teen suicide victims are suing Facebook, Instagram and others on the grounds that their algorithms were designed to addict and depress impressionable teens. And Facebook also lost a class action lawsuit that alleged that the social media giant had compromised user privacy by continuing to monitor users' online activity after they had signed off Facebook. Whether such lawsuits will alter the behavior of social media companies remains to be seen.

The viewpoints in this chapter consider who is responsible for social media behavior: not just corporate executives, but teen users themselves, parents, teachers, schools, and society at large.

Viewpoint 1

> *"It is the executives at Snapchat, Yolo, and LMK irresponsibly putting profits over the mental health of young people who ultimately need to be held accountable."*

Corporations Should Be Held Responsible for Abuses on Their Social Media Platforms

Sam Dean

In the following viewpoint, Sam Dean considers the tragic case of a teen boy who committed suicide after enduring months of anonymous, bullying messages. His mother is suing the social media companies that she says facilitated the bullying. To date, such cases have proved futile, for the law is on the side of the social media companies. But the courts have lately shown more favor to plaintiffs who argue that the sites are breaking consumer protection laws. Given that these social media sites claim to go to great lengths to protect their users, plaintiffs have argued that they are violating their own promises by allowing lethal bullying. Sam Dean is a business reporter for the Los Angeles Times *covering the technology industry in Southern California.*

"A Teen Who Was Bullied on Snapchat Died. His Mom Is Suing to Hold Social Media Liable," by Sam Dean, Los Angeles Times, May 10, 2021.

As you read, consider the following questions:

1. What are Section 230 protections for social media companies?
2. What specific promises have social media sites such as Yolo made about protecting users?
3. Why do attorneys in the Bride lawsuit believe they may have a better chance at successfully suing social media sites than they previously had?

One of the last things that Carson Bride did before taking his own life was look to his phone for help.

The 16-year-old had been receiving anonymous messages for months, according to a federal lawsuit filed Monday in California, through a popular Snapchat app called Yolo. The messages included sexual comments and taunts over specific incidents, such as the time he'd fainted in biology class at his Portland, Ore., school.

The messages had to be coming from people he knew, but the app's design made it impossible for him to know who was behind it. If he replied to the taunts, Yolo would automatically make the original message public, revealing his humiliation to the world.

His family found him dead June 23, 2020. The history on his phone showed that he had been searching for "Reveal YOLO Username Online" earlier that morning.

Now Kristin Bride, Carson's mother, is leading a lawsuit against Snap, Yolo and LMK, another anonymous messaging app built for Snapchat that the teenager used before his death. Her complaint alleges that the companies violated consumer protection law by failing to live up to their own terms of service and policies, and that anonymous messaging apps facilitate bullying to such a degree that they should be considered dangerous products.

The suit, filed Monday in federal court in the Northern District of California, seeks to form a class on behalf of the approximately 93 million U.S. users of Snapchat—a number that the company says includes 90% of all Americans ages 13 to 24—along with the

10 million users of Yolo and 1 million users of LMK. Bride's co-plaintiff in the case is the Tyler Clementi Foundation, a nonprofit formed to prevent bullying by the family of Tyler Clementi, who took his own life at age 18 in 2010 after experiencing cyber harassment by a dorm mate at Rutgers University.

Snap declined to comment on active litigation. Yolo and LMK did not respond to requests for comment.

The lawsuit seeks to have Yolo and LMK immediately banned from Snap's platform, along with any other apps that have failed to set up safeguards against cyberbullying, and seeks damages for the alleged harms and misrepresentations.

"The high school students who anonymously cyberbullied Carson will live with this tragedy for the rest of their lives," Kristin Bride said in a statement provided by Eisenberg & Baum, the law firm representing the plaintiffs. "However, it is the executives at Snapchat, Yolo, and LMK irresponsibly putting profits over the mental health of young people who ultimately need to be held accountable."

To date, those attempting to sue social media companies over their users' words and actions have met with little success. Most cases against tech companies over content posted by their users are dismissed out of hand under Section 230 of the 1996 Communications Decency Act, which states that no "interactive computer service" can be held liable for information posted by a user on that service.

But changes in the legal landscape and a novel legal argument may set this case apart.

In a ruling last week, the U.S. 9th Circuit Court of Appeals opened the door to the idea that social media companies—and Snap in particular—can be held responsible for building or enabling features that are so clearly dangerous to its users that the product is essentially defective.

That case centered on a Snapchat filter that automatically detected how fast the user was moving and let them add that number to a post on the platform. Plaintiffs in the suit argued that the feature incentivized driving at high speeds, leading to a fatal 2017 car crash in Wisconsin, in which a 17-year-old passenger pulled up Snap moments before the car hit a speed of 123 mph, then ran off the road and crashed into a tree.

The 9th Circuit reversed a lower court's decision to dismiss the case over Section 230 protections, with Judge Kim McLane Wardlaw writing that "this type of claim rests on the premise that manufacturers have a 'duty to exercise due care in supplying products that do not present unreasonable risk of injury or harm to the public.'"

In the case filed Monday, Bride and the Tyler Clementi Foundation argue that anonymous messaging features such as Yolo and LMK similarly present unreasonable risk of harm. To bolster this argument, the suit points to multiple generations of anonymous messaging apps targeted at teen users that have risen

Big Tech Exploits Kids

At the risk of understatement, the recent revelations by whistleblower Frances Haugen on how Facebook and Instagram view children were shocking. In her testimony, she claimed that Facebook's own internal research showed that the social media platform "has a serious negative harm on a significant portion of teenagers and younger children." These services expose children to online predators, and have increased the incidence of teenage eating disorders, body image issues and suicidal thoughts among teenagers.

The government has so far failed to hold Silicon Valley accountable for the dangers social media poses to children. But while existing penalties are proving insufficient, legal principles that already apply to other hazards can inspire a new legislative approach.

Fines have been federal agencies' go-to method of punishing Big Tech for profiting off child users. In early 2019 the Federal Trade Commission fined Musical.ly (now TikTok) $5.7 million for illegally collecting personal information from children. Later that year, the commission leveled the same charge against Google and YouTube and collapsed in recent years, each brought down under the weight of abuse and harassment that they enabled, such as Yik Yak, Secret and Sarahah.

The suit cites research linking anonymous harassment and teen suicide to bolster this argument, including a 2007 study that found that students who experience bullying, online or in real life, are nearly twice as likely to attempt suicide. A subsequent study in 2014 found that cyberbullying may be even more dangerous, with online bullying tripling the risk for suicidal ideation.

But the suit also pursues a line of argument that draws from consumer protection law, arguing that Snap, Yolo and LMK failed to live up to their terms of service and other commitments to users.

A recent decision in the 2nd Circuit Court of Appeals in New York City showed that this consumer protection argument might

with a $170 million penalty. To put those numbers in context, TikTok's market cap is estimated to exceed $140 billion, and Google's annual revenues exceed $180 billion. To Big Tech companies, fines are just a slap on the wrist.

Federal law, as it now stands, is of little help. Congress's primary venture into protecting kids online—the Children's Online Privacy Protection Act, passed in 1998—is primarily targeted at protecting the personal information of children (under 13) online. It requires disclaimers, limits targeted advertising and pushes websites to get parental consent before kids can sign up.

The problem is that kids can't be expected to read disclaimers (and few teens or adults do in any case). Kids still can see advertising (even if it's not targeted to them individually). And parents don't get the option to consent in part—it's all or nothing for most sites, so if a school assigns watching an online video as homework, its students will have access to almost everything else as well.

It's time for Congress to step in and update children's online protections for the 21st century.

"Stop Big Tech from Exploiting Our Kids," by Joel Thayer, Newsweek, October 26, 2021.

have legs. In that case, the plaintiff argued that the gay dating app Grindr should be held responsible for harassment he received on the app from a former boyfriend, who set up a fake account for the plaintiff and sent a stream of 1,400 strange men to his house looking for sex over the course of 10 months.

The court dismissed the case, citing Section 230 protections, and wrote that it was unclear that Grindr was in violation of its terms of service for a number of reasons. But the judge's ruling indicated that a case showing a more clear-cut violation of those terms and agreements could have merit on consumer protection grounds.

A suit filed in early April against Facebook relies on a similar strategy. The civil rights group Muslim Advocates sued the social media giant alleging that it has failed to live up to its promises to users by allowing hate speech against Muslims to proliferate on the platform unchecked.

An approach based on consumer protection laws might find traction in the court, said Jeff Kosseff, a law professor at the U.S. Naval Academy and the author of a book about Section 230, "The Twenty-Six Words That Created the Internet."

"Five years ago, I would have predicted that this case would almost definitely be dismissed" because of the internet shield law, Kosseff said, "but now I think it could really go either way.

"This is a really horrible, tragic case, and judges who are reading these cases are not completely blind to that. No matter how much case law there is, they're clearly going to be influenced by the fact these are some really terrible allegations in this complaint."

A prompt shown to first-time Yolo users warns that the app has "no tolerance for objectionable content or abusive users," and that users will be banned for inappropriate behavior. Its privacy policy warns users that the company collects user information in order to enforce that zero tolerance policy.

But after discovering the bullying Yolo messages and search history on her son's phone, Bride contacted the company through its website, sending a message about her son's cyberbullying and resulting death. Yolo never responded, according to the suit.

Months later, Bride and her husband, Tom, again tried to contact Yolo through its website and via an email address provided for reporting emergencies, demanding that the company remove the bullying users from its platform. The email carried the subject line "Our Son's Suicide—Request for Help." The emergency reporting account replied only with a bounce-back message, saying that the recipient could not be reached due to an invalid address. Two subsequent attempts to contact the company also went unanswered, according to the suit.

LMK, the other third-party app in the suit, made even stronger claims about user safety, writing in its terms of service that it would "go to great lengths to protect our community" from inappropriate usage, including using "artificial intelligence technology" and human moderation to police its content.

And Snap, the suit alleges, has failed to live up to its own promises to users by allowing these apps to run on its service.

Snap allows other companies to build apps for its platform with a set of tools called Snap Kit and makes clear in its guidelines that it actively reviews all third-party apps, noting that "encouraging or promoting violence, harassment, bullying, hate speech, threats and/or self-harm" is unacceptable, as is having "inadequate safeguards in place to prevent this type of behavior."

Those guidelines also state that any app with anonymous user-generated content is subject to a longer review process, and if a third-party app is noncompliant or violates guidelines, Snap reserves the right to remove the app from its platform.

Snap has not removed Yolo or LMK from its platform, "even though it knows or has reason to know through numerous reports that Yolo and LMK lack adequate safeguards to prevent teen users from being victimized by harassment, sexually explicit materials, and other harm," according to the suit.

VIEWPOINT 2

> *"We find that parents are more likely to talk with teens about digital safety and behavior issues, and are somewhat less likely to take a more hands-on approach to restrict or monitor their child."*

Studies Show Parents Are Active in Monitoring Teens' Online Behavior

Amanda Lenhart, Mary Madden, Aaron Smith, Kristen Purcell, and Kathryn Zickuhr

In the following viewpoint, authors from the Pew Research Center write about the results of a study of parent and teen behavior with regard to teenagers' internet use. The survey finds that a high percentage of parents, particularly those of younger teens, have discussed online social media behavior with their children. Fewer parents monitor their children's behavior through technology, yet a substantial percentage have taken steps to safeguard their teens. In addition, many coaches are active in making sure that teens have an appropriate online presence. And while some teens see parents' "friending" of their children as intrusive, others see nothing wrong with it and accept it without question. Amanda Lenhart is the Former Director of Teens and Technology Research the Internet & American Life Project. Mary Madden is a former senior researcher. Aaron Smith is Director of Data Labs. Kristen Purcell is the Associate Director for Research at the Internet & American Life Project. Kathryn Zickuhr is a former Research Associate.

As you read, consider the following questions:

1. What are some of the approaches parents have used to engage with teens on the topic of online safety?
2. How are parents becoming more vigilant in safeguarding their children online?
3. How are the habits of White and Black parents different from those of Latinx parents with regard to teens' online behavior?

Parents in the United States are still the primary gatekeepers and managers of their teens' internet experience. As discussed earlier in the report, parents are the most often cited source of advice and the biggest influence on teens' understanding of appropriate and inappropriate digital behavior. Parents are also responsible for keeping their teens safe online and offline and have a number of tools at their disposal to do so.

There are a variety of approaches to engaging with teens on the topic of online safety. Parents can talk to their teens about safe and risky online practices and about appropriate and inappropriate behavior. Parents can also answer questions that teens have and give advice in response to questions. They can also take concrete steps to monitor or check up on their teens' online activities, including the relatively low-tech techniques of checking which websites a teen has visited, viewing his or her social media profiles, or friending him or her on a social network. This monitoring might also include use of parental controls on the computer or cell phone that a teen uses.

In this study, we asked parents (and often teens as well) about whether or not they engaged in the following actions:

- Talked with you/your child about ways to use the internet and cell phones safely
- Talked with you/your child about ways to behave toward other people online or on the phone

- Talked with you/your child about what you/he or she does on the internet
- Talked with you/your child about what kinds of things should and should not be shared online or on a cell phone
- Checked to see what information was available online about your child[47]
- Checked your social network site profile[48]
- Checked which websites you/your child visited
- Friended your child on social media[49]
- Used parental controls or other means of blocking, filtering or monitoring your/your child's online activities
- Used parental controls to restrict your/your child's use of your/his or her cell phone.

In this study, we find that parents are more likely to talk with teens about digital safety and behavior issues, and are somewhat less likely to take a more hands-on approach to restrict or monitor their child. Both parents and teens confirm these tendencies.

The vast majority of parents of online teenagers have had serious conversations with their kids about the do's and don'ts of online behavior.

We asked both teens and parents about whether parents talk with their children about online safety, and overwhelmingly, both groups said that parents are talking to teens about these issues. From the teen perspective, more than four in five parents engage their kids in conversations about ways to use the internet and cell phones safely, ways to behave toward other people online or on a mobile phone, what kinds of things should and should not be shared online, and what the teen is doing online or on his or her phone. As we often see when we ask questions of both parents and teens, parents are statistically more likely than their teens to say that they talk to their child about various issues. In this case, the discussion topics that parents and teens reported differently include ways to use the internet and cell phone safely, what their child does on the internet or cell phone, and what kind of things should and should not be shared online or on a cell phone.

Virtually all parents of online teens (98%) have talked to their children about the way to behave online and cope with problems in sometimes-challenging internet realms. These important conversations do not appear to have fallen on deaf ears; when we asked teens about the conversations they had with their parents, there was considerable overlap in the topics covered. Parents and teens report that they have discussed a wide range of safety and behavioral issues that relate to online life.

94% of parents—and 88% of online teens—report discussing what kinds of things should and should not be shared online. Fully 94% of parents of online teens say they discuss what kinds of things should and should not be shared online with their child. Latino parents of online teens are somewhat less likely than whites or blacks to say they have done this. Those in households earning more than $50,000 annually are more likely than those in lower-income households to have done it.

When we asked teens about these conversations with parents, younger teens ages 12-13 are somewhat more likely than their older counterparts to report parents discussing what kinds of things should and should not be shared on a cell phone or online (93% vs. 86% of older teens).

According to teens, parents who use social media are more likely to talk with their teen about what kinds of things should and should not be shared online or on a cell phone. Teens report that parents who are friends with their teens on social media are more likely to have these conversations than parents who have not friended their child (92% vs. 79%). Parents who do not use social media are more likely to have teens who report that their parents do not talk about any online behavior or safety issues with them.

Teens who had received sexts were less likely to report parents talking with them about what kinds of things should and should not be shared on a cell phone.

93% of parents and 85% of teens say they have discussed ways to use the internet safely.

Parents of online teens ages 12-13 are more likely than parents of older kids to have had these conversations about how to use the internet safely. Among parents who are friends with their teen on a social network site, 97% report that they have talked about these issues with their child, while 87% of parents who do not use social network sites at all have done the same.

When the question was asked of teens, younger teens 12-13 are more likely to say their parents discuss ways to use the internet and cell phones safely (89% vs. 83% of older teens). Girls are also more likely than boys to report their parents talking with them about digital safety (89% vs. 81% of boys). Younger girls are more likely to have these conversations with their parents than older boys, with the data trend visible even more strongly among younger girls who have a cell phone and use texting.

Teens who think peers are mostly unkind on social network sites and those who have been victims of online cruelty are also more likely to say that their parents have talked with them about ways to use the internet and cell phones safely (94% vs. 83% for those who think peers are unkind vs. kind, and a similar 94% vs. 83% for those who have and have not been victims of online cruelty).

87% of parents have discussed with their teen what she or he has been doing online.

A total of 87% of parents (and a slightly smaller 82% of teens) say that parents have talked with their teen about what she or he has been doing online. Mothers are more likely than fathers to have done this (91% vs. 82%).

When the question is asked of teens, online teens who do not use social network sites are more likely to report having this discussion with their parents than those who use social media.

Among social media users, teens who keep their online social media profile private are more likely than teens who have an entirely public profile to report having talked with their parents about what they do online or on their cell phone—87% of private profile owners say they have talked with their parents about what they do online compared with 73% of those with a public profile. Similarly, those who have experienced online cruelty also are more likely to report that a parent talked with them about what they do on the internet or their phone.

87% of parents have suggested ways to behave toward other people online.

Parents of online girls are more likely than parents of boys to say they have discussed this with their teen. Among teens asked this question, those teens who have received sexually suggestive texts and those who have experienced any type of bullying in the past 12 months—whether online, on the phone, or in-person—are less likely than teens who had not received or experienced these things to say that their parents had talked with them about how to behave online.

Parental monitoring: Non-technical steps are preferred by parents.

Beyond simply talking with teens about online safety and civility, parents and other adult caregivers have other actions and technical tools at their disposal to help maintain their awareness of their child's online activities.

Overall, parents are more likely to favor less technical steps for monitoring their child's online behavior. More than three-quarters (77%) of parents say that they have checked to see what websites their child has visited. Two-thirds of parents of online teens have checked to see what information was available online about their child. More than six in ten teens report that they know their parents have checked their social media profile, and 41% of parents of online teens have friended their child on a social network site.

66% of parents of online teens have checked to see what information about their teen is available on the internet.

In the age of widespread use of social network sites by teens, many parents have become vigilant about monitoring their child's activities online, the information that is available about them, and their comings and goings on social network sites.

Two-thirds of parents (66%) say they have searched for their child's digital footprints online. Mothers who use the internet (75%) are considerably more likely than fathers (55%) to report checking on their teenage child's digital reputation, and higher-income parents are more likely to do this than those who live in households with more modest incomes. White and black parents are more likely to report this type of searching than Latino parents, as are parents with greater levels of education.

The oldest girls ages 14-17 are more likely to have their parents search for information about them online than the youngest boys, with 72% of the parents of older girls searching, compared with 55% of the parents of younger boys. Social media and use of mobile phones also relate to parents searching online for information about their child. Teens with cell phones, teens who have sent and received sexts, as well as social media users are all also more likely to have their parents check and see what information is available about them online.

Parents who themselves have experience using social media are more likely to perform these checks. The most active parents checking on their child's digital material are those who have connected with their children via social network sites.

Parents are becoming more vigilant in monitoring their teen's online browsing.

The proportion of parents who say they check on the websites their child visits online has risen since 2006. Some 77% of the parents of online teens say they do this, compared with 65% who said they did so in our 2006 survey.

White parents of online teens (83%) are more likely to check the websites of their browsing teens than black parents (75%) or

Latino parents (64%). Parents in higher-income households and those with at least a high school diploma are also more likely than others to check up on their teen's online travels. The age and gender of the teenager are not associated with this kind of parental vigilance. The parents who have become friends with their teen on social network sites are also more likely to have done this.

Checking the social network site profile of teen[50]

Nearly two-thirds (61%) of social media-using teens report that their parents have checked their social network site profile. White and black teens were more likely than Latino teens to report that their parents had checked their social media profile. According to teens, parents with a high school education and above were more likely than parents with lower levels of education to check the content of the teen's online profile. Teens who had directly experienced online cruelty were also a bit more likely than those who had not to have parents who checked their online profile.

39% of parents have friended their teenager on social network sites, but being connected to a child that way does not necessarily ward off problems.

Taking monitoring social media a step further than simply checking their child's profile or web usage, some 39% of all parents of teens are friends with or otherwise connected to their children via social network sites. That translates into 45% of online parents. We arrive at that overall figure by noting that 87% of parents of teens use the internet. Of them, 67% use social network sites. Of those parents who use social network sites, 84% say they have children who use social network sites. Finally, 80% of those social media-using parents whose teens also use social media have friended or connected with that child via social media.

Interestingly, there are no notable demographic differences among parents who make this kind of online connection with their teenagers and those who do not—either by gender, race, age, or class.

Parents who friend their teens on social media are more likely to implement other online safety or parental control measures.

Parents who have friended their teen on social media are more likely to use some forms of parental controls. Nearly two-thirds (63%) of parents who friend their teens use parental controls, while only 31% of parents who are not social media friends with their teens use these tools on their computer. Those who connect with their kids via social network sites are also considerably more likely than others to have checked on the material that is available online about their teenager: 85% of the parents in this group have checked to see what information is available online about their child, compared with 45% of the parents who belong to a social network site but have not friended their teen. However, parents who friend their teen are just as likely as those who do not to say they use parental controls on their child's cell phone (33% vs. 29%).

Friending parents on social media is associated with an increased likelihood of parent-child conflict over social media.

Friending a teen on social media may have some protective effects, but it is not without its costs, too. Teens whose parents report that they are friends with their child on social network sites are more likely than teens who aren't friends with their parents to say that they had a problem with their parents because of an experience on social media (18% vs. 5%).

Teens themselves have mixed feelings about being friended by their parents on Facebook. Some teens saw it as a normal part of a parent's job and were relatively unbothered by it:

- MIDDLE SCHOOL GIRL: [Parents] should just check in every once in a while.
- MIDDLE SCHOOL BOY: I friended my mom without even thinking about it. For one thing, she's never on Facebook. And for another, I don't really care if she sees what I do. I'm

not going out and drinking or whatever with bunches of people I don't know, so she can look.

Others thought parents friending teens was more of an affront:

- MIDDLE SCHOOL GIRL: My mother is [on Facebook]. She doesn't have me as a friend. That's crazy serious.

And some teens explained that other people in their lives like coaches and cousins kept an eye on them through Facebook:

- MIDDLE SCHOOL BOY: My parents check my wall. Sometimes even coaches check my wall.
- MIDDLE SCHOOL GIRL: My coach is my [Facebook] friend…he's like 'oh, bring the spikes' or 'oh our uniforms are here.' He posts random stuff on my wall. Our whole track team has their own page.

More than half of parents say they use parental controls to manage teens' internet access; another third use parental controls on teens' mobile phones.

Parents are also using hardware and software-based tools to monitor their teens' online activities or block them from accessing certain content. These tools can be standalone software that is purchased or downloaded, or can be built into a browser or a computer operating system. More than half (54%) of parents say they use parental controls or other means of filtering or monitoring their child's computer-based online activities, while 39% of online teens report that their parents use this type of software or feature in a browser or operating system to manage their teen's computer-based internet experience.

White parents (58%) and black parents (61%) are more likely than Latino parents (35%) to have done this. And the parents who have become friends on social network sites with their children are also more likely to report using parental controls.

Teens with parents who have been to college are also more likely to have parent controls in-use than teens with parents with a high school diploma. In a similar vein, teens from the lowest income households (under $30,000 annually) were much less likely to report use of parental controls than teens from the highest income households (more than $75,000 annually). There are no differences by gender or age in the report of use of parental controls by teens.

About a third of parents use parental controls on their teens' mobile phone.

Given that so many mobile phones now incorporate easy internet access, and because of the ways that information in the form of text, photos, or videos can be recorded and shared with others on phones, companies have responded to parent and policy maker requests for parental controls for phones on family plans.[51] Teens and parents report that parents are taking advantage of these controls for cell phones, with 34% of parents reporting use of parental controls to restrict mobile phone use and 19% of teens reporting their parents' use of the tools. Two percent of teens do not know if their parents use the controls. Parents of younger teenage boys (those ages 12-13) are the most likely to have restricted their teen's cell use.

17% of all parents use both forms of parental controls; 41% do not use any parental controls.

Half (54%) of parents whose child uses the internet have used parental controls to restrict access to or content on the internet, and 34% of parents whose child uses a cell phone have used parental controls on their child's device. When looking at all parents of teens, regardless of their computer or phone ownership or use, 42% of parents use one parental control, either for internet or on a cell phone, and 17% of parents say they use parental controls in both locations. Another 41% of all parents say that they do not use any parental controls. According to a another recent study, the bulk of the parents who do not use parental controls report that they feel they are unnecessary, either because of rules already in place, or because they trust their child to be safe.[52]

Notes

47. Asked only of parents who use the internet – not asked of teens.
48. Asked only of teens who use social network sites or Twitter.
49. Asked only of parents who use social media and had a child who uses social media – not asked of teens.
50. This question was asked only of teens – about their parents' activity.

77% of teens have a cell in this study. The cell phone data from the study will be treated more fully in a later Pew Internet report.

52. Hart Research (2011) "Who Needs Parental Controls? A Survey of Awareness, Attitudes and Use of Online Parental Controls." Family Online Safety Institute, Washington, DC. September 14, 2011. http://www.fosi.org/images/stories/research/ fosi_hart_survey-report.pdf

VIEWPOINT 3

"Legislation proposed in Congress earlier this year would require consent for collecting data from teenagers."

Technology Companies Are Addressing Social Media Privacy Concerns

Andrea Vittorio

In the following viewpoint, Andrea Vittorio argues that, spurred on by lawmakers, social media companies have begun to institute measures to give teenagers more control over their own privacy. Social media companies collect information on their users, but there are already laws in the U.S. that prohibit companies from doing so for younger social media enthusiasts. Lawmakers are looking at extending these protections for older teens. Child advocates argue that stricter measures are needed because some teens lie about their age to evade privacy controls. Andrea Vittorio is a Senior Reporter at Bloomberg Industry Group.

As you read, consider the following questions:

1. How do TikTok's privacy settings work for teenagers?
2. What specific changes are lawmakers looking into?
3. How are company spokespersons responding to proposed additional privacy measures?

Tech companies including TikTok, Alphabet Inc., and Facebook Inc. are tightening privacy controls for teenagers as social media platforms feel policy pressure over protections for younger users.

Short-video platform TikTok, which is popular among teens, is changing privacy settings for users ages 13 to 17 to give them more control over who they share videos and messages with, the company announced in a blog post.

TikTok already makes accounts belonging to users under age 16 private by default, meaning only someone that they approve as a follower can view their videos. Features like messaging directly with other TikTok users are reserved for users who are 16 and older. The new controls for teens ages 13 to 17 build on existing measures by adding privacy prompts for video posts and downloads, along with a new default for direct messages.

TikTok's measures come on the heels of similar moves to make teen accounts on Alphabet's YouTube and Facebook's Instagram more private by default.

Tech companies are likely acting in response to new design standards for children's privacy in the U.K. and a legislative proposal targeting teen privacy in the U.S., according to Josh Golin, executive director of children's advocacy group Fairplay.

The U.K.'s so-called age appropriate design code directs online services to build in privacy protections by default and to explain settings in ways that children would understand. Enforcement of the code begins in September.

"You can clearly see the hand of the age appropriate design code in all three of these announcements," Golin said of the recent moves by TikTok, Google, and Facebook.

U.S. lawmakers are also showing interest in teen privacy that could lead to new rules for companies to follow. Legislation proposed in Congress earlier this year would require consent for collecting data from teenagers.

Age Ranges

In the U.S., children under age 13 are subject to the Children's Online Privacy Protection Act. The law, known as COPPA, gives parents control over what information online platforms can collect about their kids.

Companies that violate COPPA can face fines from the Federal Trade Commission. TikTok reached a record $5.7 million settlement with the agency in 2019 for not safeguarding the data of app users who were under 13. Google's YouTube was also subject to a $170 million children's privacy pact with the commission.

A bill from Sens. Edward Markey (D-Mass.) and Bill Cassidy (R-La.) would extend privacy protections to teenagers ages 13 to

Inconclusive Data

On Tuesday, Facebook whistleblower Frances Haugen testified before a Senate panel. The hearing's focus was advertised as "protecting kids online."

"I believe that Facebook's products harm children," she said in her opening statement, saying that the documents she published proved that Facebook's "profit optimizing machine is generating self-harm and self-hate—especially for vulnerable groups, like teenage girls." Facebook spokesperson Andy Stone noted on Twitter during the hearing that Haugen "did not work on child safety or Instagram or research these issues and has no direct knowledge of the topic from her work at Facebook."

Researchers have worked for decades to tease out the relationship between teen media use and mental health. Although there is debate, they tend to agree that the evidence we've seen so far is complex, contradictory and ultimately inconclusive. That is equally true of Facebook's internal marketing data, leaked by Haugen, as it is of the validated studies on the topic.

The leaked Facebook research consists of opinion surveys and interviews. Facebook asked teens about their impressions of Instagram's effect on their body image, mental health and other issues.

15. In the House, Rep. Kathy Castor (D-Fla.) has floated a bill, H.R. 4801, with similar protections for teens up to 17.

The Senate bill, S. 1628, also would raise legal expectations for social media companies to know that children are on their platform. Children's advocates argue that stricter standards are needed, because some children lie about their age to create accounts on platforms like TikTok and Facebook's photo-sharing app Instagram.

The U.K.'s design code, which covers children under 18, separates them into different age groups depending on their maturity level. Ages 13 to 15 are considered early teens, while those between 16 and 17 are approaching adulthood, according to the code.

That reliance on self-reporting—the teens' own opinions—as a single indicator of harm is a problem, says Candice Odgers, a psychologist who studies adolescence at University of California, Irvine and Duke University. That's because teenagers are already primed by media coverage, and the disapproval of adults, to believe that social media is bad for them.

Odgers was a coauthor of a study conducted in 2015 and published in 2020 that found exactly this. "If you ask teens if they are addicted/harmed by social media or their phones, the vast majority say yes," she tells NPR. "But if you actually do the research and connect their use to objective measures ... there is very little to no connection." With the exception of a small increase in behavior problems, her study found no real world connections between smartphone or social media use and several different measures of psychological distress and well-being. "At the population level," the paper concluded, "there was little evidence that digital technology access and use is negatively associated with young adolescents' well-being."

"Facebook's Own Data Is Not as Conclusive as You Think About Teens and Mental Health," by Anya Kamenetz, NPR.org, October 6, 2021.

TikTok's new privacy controls are specific to teens in those age bands.

"They clearly had this code in mind," said Phyllis Marcus, a partner at Hunton Andrews Kurth who previously led the FTC's program for children's privacy online. Other online platforms are expected to adopt measures like these as policymakers in the U.K. and U.S. shine a light on safeguarding children online, Marcus said.

Default Settings

TikTok's measures are meant to help teens understand available settings, according to the post from Alexandra Evans, the company's head of child safety public policy, and Aruna Sharma, global head of privacy.

The platform, owned by China's ByteDance Ltd., is adding a pop-up when teens under age 16 post their first video, asking them to choose who can watch it. Teens on TikTok can continue to decide their audience for each video going forward.

"The process of making a TikTok is fun and creative—choosing music, picking effects, and getting the transitions right—but it is just as important to choose who that video will be shared with," the post from Evans and Sharma said.

When a teen between the ages of 16 and 17 joins TikTok, their account will be set in a way that requires them to choose a sharing option before being able to message directly with other users. Teens in that age bracket will also see a pop-up asking them to confirm their settings before other TikTok users can download their videos.

YouTube is likewise making videos uploaded by users ages 13 to 17 private by default in the coming weeks, while Instagram is already defaulting teens younger than 16 into private accounts.

TikTok also announced that it's limiting how late at night its app sends push notifications to teens.

That shift "seems to fit in with" what would be required under another piece of legislation from Markey, according to Ariel

Fox Johnson, senior counsel for global policy at the nonprofit Common Sense, which researches and rates online platforms used by children.

The bill, S. 3411, would ban push alerts that encourage kids and young teens to spend more time on an app.

Viewpoint 4

> *"Facebook, Instagram, Google, YouTube, Twitter, and other platforms frequently accelerate the viral distribution of extreme content because it generates greater user engagement, which translates into billions of dollars in advertisements."*

Social Media Platforms Need to Self-Regulate

Michael A. Cusumano, David B. Yoffie, and Annabelle Gawer

In the following viewpoint, Michael A. Cusumano, David B. Yoffie, and Annabelle Gawer consider how big and powerful social media companies such as Facebook have become, and observe that their size and scope make it extremely difficult for outsiders or governments to regulate them. The authors consider three proposed options for regulation but reject these measures as impractical. They then suggest how social media companies might self-regulate. Michael A. Cusumano is the SMR Distinguished Professor and the Deputy Dean at the MIT Sloan School of Management. David B. Yoffie is the Max and Doris Starr Professor of International Business Administration at Harvard Business School. Annabelle Gawer is the Chaired Professor in Digital Economy and Director of the Centre of Digital Economy at Surrey Business School.

"Pushing Social Media Platforms to Self-Regulate," by Michael A. Cusumano, David B. Yoffie, and Annabelle Gawer, The Regulatory Review, January 3, 2022. Reprinted by permission.

As you read, consider the following questions:

1. What three proposals for dealing with social media companies do the authors consider impractical?
2. What three alternatives do the authors suggest?
3. Why are "episodic" fines unlikely to work in curtailing inappropriate behavior on social media platforms?

Online platforms can be "double-edged swords," generating spectacular economics while offering a forum for bad actors and bad behavior. To fix the dark side of platforms, only a combination of government regulation and pressure for companies to self-regulate has a chance to curb the extremes in social media. U.S. Supreme Court Justice Clarence Thomas has hinted at a similar position.

Although the challenges facing social media are global and require multinational solutions, we focus here mainly on the United States. We start by clarifying the problem we are trying to solve. On the one hand, social media platforms have an incentive problem. Facebook, Instagram, Google, YouTube, Twitter, and other platforms frequently accelerate the viral distribution of extreme content because it generates greater user engagement, which translates into billions of dollars in advertisements.

The more outrageous the content—for example, stories of grand conspiracies around the U.S. presidential election, the coronavirus, and COVID-19 vaccines—the greater the profit opportunity.

Yes, the social media companies have "terms of service" that allow them to delete harmful or illegal content. But there are no financial incentives for these firms to police themselves.

On the other hand, the volume of social media content—four billion videos are viewed on Facebook alone each day—makes it difficult and expensive, although not impossible, to track, curate, or edit so many postings.

We have been studying and writing about digital platforms since they first emerged in the 1990s. Our research has led us to conclude that many of the proposals being discussed in the press and the U.S. Congress are unlikely to work. Let us consider them one by one.

One option is to break up Facebook. This option would reduce Facebook's market power, but it does not solve any of the incentive problems or conflict of interest issues identified by Frances Haugen, the former Facebook employee and whistleblower. Even if Facebook, Instagram, and WhatsApp returned to separate companies, each application would still be a huge, powerful network with no new incentives to stop bad behavior. Similar problems would persist if YouTube were detached from Google.

Another option is for the federal government to regulate social media algorithms directly. This option, which Haugen proposed, is possible—but would be difficult to execute for technical reasons. Social media and search algorithms are designed using artificial intelligence technology. The algorithms are difficult for outsiders and even the software developers themselves to pull apart and alter, let alone fully understand. Furthermore, these algorithms are based on machine learning and big data. They continually evolve as users interact with the platforms billions of times a day. Putting in a bureaucratic change-control process monitored by government officials or even expert special masters—as occurred with the Microsoft antitrust trial settlement—would likely freeze the technology and put a damper on innovation.

A third option would be for lawmakers to eliminate Section 230. This change would get rid of the 1996 law that protects online platforms from civil liabilities for content they disseminate. But Section 230 distinguishes the platforms from publishers, the latter who are fully responsible for their content. As such, the law remains fundamental to the operations of all online platforms. We want these internet businesses to continue to be as open as possible to innovation and to facilitate freedom of expression in user-generated content—without being legally liable for each of the billions of posts on their sites.

A better alternative would be to combine government regulations that alter incentives and put more pressure on social media companies to do more self-regulation. We offer three suggestions.

First, the U.S. government should require all social media platforms to abide strictly by their own "terms of service," vesting enforcement power over these terms with the Federal Communications Commission (FCC), Federal Trade Commission (FTC), or even the Securities and Exchange Commission (SEC). These terms already give social media companies the ability to curate content or shut down accounts when they see misuse of their platforms. For example, Facebook has a set of "community standards" comprising a long list of potentially prohibited content, including posts considered to encourage violence and criminal behavior, child or sexual exploitation, hate speech, false news, and intellectual property violations.

Having terms of service is not enough, however. The federal government needs to make sure that social media firms adhere to their publicly stated terms of service and other standards. One way to force adherence would be government lawsuits or civil litigation—with fines levied against not only the companies, but also against their CEOs, other executives, and members of their boards of directors. Just as the Sarbanes-Oxley Act of 2002 made officers and directors personally liable for financial statements, new regulations could make Mark Zuckerberg and the Facebook board liable for failures to implement their terms of service.

Second, Congress, with the cooperation of the U.S. Department of Justice, should revise Section 230. We suggest that the revisions make it possible to hold the online platforms accountable for profits they earn from deliberately disseminating harmful content. The companies could then become open to civil lawsuits or specific FCC, FTC, SEC, or Justice Department actions. Since Facebook and Alphabet, Google's parent company, collectively earned $69 billion in net income in 2020, episodic fines are unlikely to alter behavior—as we have seen with European antitrust fines against Google or the $5 billion FTC fine levied against Facebook. It should be possible, however, to force the platforms to identify profits gained from advertisements tied to these viral posts and then to have those monies clawed back as fines. Those numbers could be very large.

Finally, any additional government regulation should be administered in a way that promotes more effective self-regulation, as occurred with movie ratings and advertisements for tobacco, alcohol, pornography, terrorist recruitment, or self-preferencing in airline flight listings during the 1960s and 1970s. The technology that digital platforms use is too complex and fast-changing, and the content too vast, to rely only on government monitoring.

Historically, when new, complex technologies arise and new industries emerge, a credible threat of intrusive government regulation triggers many companies to regulate their own operations. In industries such as movies and video games, the threat of government intervention spurred coalitions of firms to establish content standards and codes of conduct—including content rating systems—which have worked reasonably well. This coalition approach could work with social media platforms.

Ultimately, accountable self-regulation is good for business: Social media platforms need to take more responsibility for their impact on the world, lest they run the risk of continuing to damage essential common resources for information and commerce—the internet itself, and user trust in digital content.

Viewpoint 5

> *"Social scientists like myself have been warning for years that the ubiquity of social media might be at the root of the growing mental health crisis for teens."*

Facebook Knew About Teen Social Media Concerns and Refused to Act

Jean Twenge

In this viewpoint, Jean Twenge claims that, despite public denials, Facebook executives knew that Instagram had negative effects on teens. Moreover, she writes that Facebook's own research showed that increased regulation would help alleviate the problem. Twenge suggests that such regulation might include age restrictions on users, such as barring those under 16. But she acknowledges that enforcement might be difficult, as many teens simply lie about their age. Until social media companies take more responsibility, it is up to parents and teens themselves to regulate teen social media use. Jean Twenge is Professor of Psychology at San Diego State University. Her books include iGen: Why Today's Super-Connected Kids Are Growing Up Less Rebellious, More Tolerant, Less Happy—and Completely Unprepared for Adulthood.

"Facebook's Own Internal Documents Offer a Blueprint for Making Social Media Safer for Teens," by Jean Twenge, The Conversation, October 7, 2021. https://theconversation.com/facebooks-own-internal-documents-offer-a-blueprint-for-making-social-media-safer-for-teens-169080.

As you read, consider the following questions:

1. What are some examples Twenge gives of Facebook denying its culpability in increasing teen depression?
2. Besides age restrictions, what are some modifications of teen social media use that Twenge suggests might be useful?
3. Why does Twenge believe that teens under 16 should be banned from social media?

Right at the time social media became popular, teen mental health began to falter. Between 2010 and 2019, rates of depression and loneliness doubled in the U.S. and globally, suicide rates soared for teens in the U.S. and emergency room admissions for self-harm tripled among U.S. 10- to 14-year-old girls. Social scientists like myself have been warning for years that the ubiquity of social media might be at the root of the growing mental health crisis for teens.

Yet when Facebook CEO Mark Zuckerberg was asked during a congressional hearing in March to acknowledge the connection between social media and these troubling mental health trends, he replied, "I don't think that the research is conclusive on that."

Just six months later, The Wall Street Journal reported that Facebook had been doing its own research for years on the negative effects of Instagram, the company's photo-sharing app popular with teens and young adults. Six internal documents summarizing the research, leaked by a whistle-blower, were posted in full on Sept. 29, 2021.

The details in the 209 pages are revealing. They suggest not only that Facebook knew how Instagram could be harmful, but that the company also was aware of possible solutions to mitigate those harms. Facebook's own research strongly suggests that social media should be subject to more stringent regulation and include more guardrails to protect the mental health of its users.

There are two primary ways the company can do this: enforcing time limits and increasing the minimum age of users.

A Ticking Time Bomb for Mental Health

Academic research shows that the more hours a day a teen spends on social media, the more likely she or he is to be depressed or to self-harm.

That's important because many teens, especially girls, spend large amounts of time on social media.

One study in the U.K. found that one-quarter of 15-year-old girls spent more than five hours a day using social media—and 38% of those girls were clinically depressed. Comparatively, among girls who used social media less than one hour a day, only 15% were depressed.

Although the internal Facebook research didn't examine links between time on Instagram and mental health, they did ask teens about what were, in their view, the worst aspects of Instagram. One of the things teens disliked the most about the app was how much time they spent on it.

Teens, the report said, had "an addict's narrative about their use. … They wish they could spend less time caring about it but they can't help themselves."

They knew they were spending too much time online, but had a hard time controlling how much time they spent. One-third of teens suggested Instagram should remind them to take a break or encourage them to get off the app.

That would be a step in the right direction, but simple nudges might not be enough to get teens to close the app and keep it closed. And while parents can already set time limits using the parental controls included on most smartphones, many of them don't know how to use these controls or are unaware how much time teens are spending on social media.

So better regulations might need to put teeth into time limits, such as limiting the number of hours teens under 18 can spend on social media apps. A blackout period overnight might also be useful, as many teens use their smartphones at night when they should be sleeping.

ID, Please

One internal Facebook study of more than 50,000 people from 10 countries found that half of teen girls compare their appearance to others' on Instagram. Those appearance-based comparisons, the study found, peaked when users were 13 to 18 and were much less common among adult women.

This is key, as body image issues seem to be one of the biggest reasons why social media use is linked to depression among teen girls. It also dovetails with research I reported in my book, "iGen," finding that social media use is more strongly linked to unhappiness among younger teens than older ones.

This suggests another avenue for regulation: age minimums. A 1998 law called the Children's Online Privacy Protection Rule already sets the age minimum for social media accounts at 13. That limit is problematic for two reasons. First, 13 is a developmentally challenging time, right as boys and girls are going through puberty and bullying is at its peak.

Second, the age minimum is not regularly enforced. Kids 12 and under can simply lie about their age to sign up for an account, and they're rarely kicked off the platform for being underage. During a Facebook event with Instagram head Adam Mosseri, the young celebrity JoJo Siwa noted she had been using Instagram since she was 8 years old, forcing Mosseri to acknowledge that it's easy to lie about your age.

The problem is how to enforce an age limit online for a population that is too young for IDs. Raising the minimum age to create a social media account to 16, 17 or 18 could solve two problems at once: It would prevent kids from signing up until they're a bit more developed and mature, and it would be easier to enforce. For example, potential users might be asked to submit a photo of their state-issued ID, which most teens have by 16.

Verifying age would also make it easier to construct a safer app for younger users that might, say, hide follower counts or restrict access to celebrity accounts, both of which Facebook's research found negatively impacted girls' body images.

Curtailing That Fear of Missing Out

It's tempting to think regulations like these would cause teens to riot in the streets—after all, they love keeping up with their friends on social media. But the teens interviewed by Facebook for its internal research were well aware of social media's downsides.

"The reason why our generation is so messed up and has higher anxiety and depression than our parents' is because we have to deal with social media. Everyone feels like they have to be perfect," one teen girl told the researchers. Other teens have spoken publicly about the negative effects of social media.

More stringent regulation would help with another issue teens know all too well: the unwritten mandate to use social media or be left out.

"Young people are acutely aware that Instagram can be bad for their mental health yet are compelled to spend time on the app for fear of missing out," Facebook's internal research concluded.

If age limits were enforced, the peer pressure of being on social media would vanish; no or few classmates would be there. Regulating time on the app could also help if teens knew their friends wouldn't constantly be online.

Facebook's research demonstrates something else: The company was aware of the issues with Instagram but chose not to set these limits itself. Congress is now considering taking action.

Until they do, it will be up to parents and teens themselves to set limits. That won't be easy, but teens will be safer for it.

Periodical and Internet Sources Bibliography

The following articles have been selected to supplement the diverse views presented in this chapter.

Kara Alaimo, "It's time for social networks to take a close look in the mirror," CNN. October 27, 2021. https://www.cnn.com/2021/10/27/opinions/facebook-papers-social-media-senate-hearings-alaimo/index.html.

Alan Blotcky, "What's TikTok doing to our kids? Concerns from a clinical psychologist," *New York Daily News*. November 18, 2021. https://www.nydailynews.com/opinion/ny-oped-whats-tiktok-doing-to-our-kids-20211118-32kx365w2ja6rhnoe2aoorkbpi-story.html.

Christina Caron, "Worried About Your Teen on Social Media? Here's How to Help," *The New York Times*, September 21, 2021. https://www.nytimes.com/2021/09/21/well/family/teens-social-media-help.html.

Jonathan Haidt and Jean M. Twenge, "This Is Our Chance to Pull Teenagers Out of the Smartphone Trap," *The New York Times*. July 31, 2021. https://www.nytimes.com/2021/07/31/opinion/smartphone-iphone-social-media-isolation.html.

Barth Keck, "OP-ED: It's Time To Combat Social Media That Target and Endanger Kids," CT News Junkie. October 4, 2021. https://ctnewsjunkie.com/2021/10/04/op-ed-its-time-to-combat-social-media-that-target-and-endanger-kids/.

Nancy Kim, "Op-Ed: Think Facebook is invincible? Here's how the social media giant can be held accountable," *Los Angeles Times*. November 13, 2021. https://www.latimes.com/opinion/story/2021-11-13/facebook-lawsuits-section-230.

Stuart Koman and Robert J. Keane "Opinion: Our children are being damaged by social media. Does anyone care?" *Hartford Courant*. November 15, 2021. https://www.courant.com/opinion/op-ed/hc-op-social-media-eating-disorders-20211115-2t337pigyjffdivuhzhudprurm-story.html.

Thomas D. Lehrman and Brad Wilcox, "No Instagram or TikTok Without Parental Consent," *The Wall Street Journal*. February

23, 2022. https://www.wsj.com/articles/no-instagram-without-parental-consent-big-tech-social-media-minor-child-know-your-customer-laws-privacy-protection-11645650552.

Colleen McClain, "56% of Americans oppose the right to sue social media companies for what users post," Pew Research Center. July 1, 2021. https://www.pewresearch.org/fact-tank/2021/07/01/56-of-americans-oppose-the-right-to-sue-social-media-companies-for-what-users-post/.

Emma McCarthy, "Op-Ed: We are the ones failing our teens, not social media," *Chicago Tribune*. December 9, 2021. https://www.chicagotribune.com/opinion/commentary/ct-opinion-social-media-kids-mental-health-parents-20211209-fur6vxak2rauliqvwcj2ed6idy-story.html.

Megan McCluskey, "States Could Let Parents Sue Big Tech for Addicting Kids. Here's What That Really Means." *Time*. March 22, 2022. https://time.com/6158294/california-social-media-platform-duty-children-act/.

Annika Olson, "Opinion: It's Time to Hold Social Media Platforms Accountable," *The Austin Chronicle*. January 14, 2022. https://www.austinchronicle.com/columns/2022-01-14/opinion-its-time-to-hold-social-media-platforms-accountable/.

Marguerite Reardon, "Section 230: How it shields Facebook and why Congress wants changes," Cnet. October 6, 2021. https://www.cnet.com/news/politics/section-230-how-it-shields-facebook-and-why-congress-wants-changes/.

Adela Suliman "Mother of 11-year-old who died by suicide sues social media firms Meta and Snap," *The Washington Post*. January 22, 2022. https://www.washingtonpost.com/nation/2022/01/22/selena-rodriguez-suicide-meta-snap-lawsuit/.

OPPOSING VIEWPOINTS® SERIES

Chapter 3

Is Cyberbullying of Teenagers a Serious Problem?

Chapter Preface

Bullying is age-old and universal. Go to any zoo and you will see certain apes bully others. In 2019, visitors to Germany's Wuppertal Zoo were horrified to see one bonobo ape, who was new to that zoo, being viciously bullied by the longtime occupants. An online petition to remove the poor bonobo garnered hundreds of thousands of signatures worldwide. But the zoo itself was not swayed: aggression against a male bonobo ape, they said, was common during integration.

As is well known, humans too, can be bullies. Today, on the internet, we see videos of bullies on airplanes, bullies in supermarkets, bullies in fast food establishments. Though bullying is not exclusive to men, research shows that male bullies are typically even more intimidating and violent. Physically stronger human males have been pushing around those perceived as weaker since the dawn of humanity: in tribes, in neighborhoods, in school, at recess, over the phone, and anyplace else where two humans can communicate.

Then came the internet, and, shortly after, social media. And though the various types of bullying have remained the same, the internet proved a fertile ground for growing the act of bullying into an art form. No longer could a victim close the front door or hang up the phone on a bully. The internet provided 24/7, 365 days-a-year access to victims. Yes, victims could shut off computers or block callers on mobile phones, but the harassment was always waiting for the next time they logged on. "Cyber bullies can hide behind a mask of anonymity online and do not need direct physical access to their victims to do unimaginable harm," says Anna Maria Chavez, former head of The Girl Scouts of America.

The platforms for cyberbullying are myriad. Social media sites such as Facebook, TikTok, Instagram, Reddit, and others provide easy access to potential victims. Cyberbullies can text, email, or message their victims. Given that well over 90 percent of teens are now active online, potential bullies and victims are nearly limitless.

The types of internet bullying also vary widely. Cyberbullying can take the form of exclusion, that is, leaving someone out of a group purposely; outing or doxxing (where personal information about a victim is revealed); harassment; cyberstalking; trolling; and much more. When cyberbullies want to attack, they are only limited by their own creativity.

Is all of this just common human behavior? Are humans no better than bonobos, who are only following their instincts? And, if so, should society just let nature take its course? In a civilized society, the answer is no. We are not bonobos, though some people act as if they are. It is up to society to protect its members, and, specifically, its weakest members. Parents, friends, teachers, school administrators, online organizations, and law enforcement must all get involved in combatting bullying.

But oftentimes, victims of bullying are afraid to speak up, out of fear of retribution from the bullies, or out of embarrassment. And well-meaning organizations, including anti-bullying groups and school administrations, will often merely post information to help victims while ignoring more effective boots-on-the-ground interventions. Bullying happens at a person-to-person level, even on social media. Bullies are at their worst when they fear no consequences. Their behavior must be combatted actively, and bullies must be given consequences—whether at home, or in school, or by law enforcement—that are severe enough to discourage further inappropriate behavior. As South African human-rights activist Desmond Tutu has said, "If you are neutral in situations of injustice, you have chosen the side of the oppressor."

Viewpoint 1

> *"An empathetic child will not bully. Avid readers are not bullies."*

Social Media Makes Bullying Worse

Yrsa Sigurdardottir

In the following viewpoint, Yrsa Sigurdardottir writes about how a case of internet bullying that resulted in the suicide of a young boy inspired her most recent novel. Sigurdardottir is haunted by the death, and anger drove her to write her book. The author offers suggestions for dealing with cyberbullies. One is to focus more on the bully and less on the victim. Asking the victim to change will not alter the behavior of the cyberbully. Another suggestion is to encourage children to read. Reading promotes empathy, and empathic humans tend not to bully others. Yrsa Sigurdardottir is a renowned crime novelist and director of one of Iceland's largest engineering firms.

As you read, consider the following questions:

1. Why was there no Icelandic word for bullying until recently?
2. What are some specific suggestions the author makes for dealing with cyberbullies?
3. Why wouldn't it have been practical for Sigurdardottir to dedicate her novel, *The Absolution*, to the bullies?

"Bullying Has Always Been Bad. Social Media Makes It Worse." By Yrsa Sigurdardottir, Lit Hub, February 24, 2020. Reprinted by permission.

Although Iceland is a wonderful country and a very well-meaning society, it is by no means devoid of all social ills. Like every society, we have our share of problems, and there are plenty of individuals that step outside the borders of ethical behavior and/or the law of the land. Being a Nordic nation, we do our best to address such issues gently—sometimes countermeasures work, sometimes they do not. Unfortunately, the consequences of human behavior combined with modern trends are often extremely complex and not easily fixed with band aids, through discussion, or with regulations.

One such glaring social cancer is bullying. Before I sat down to write The Absolution there had been a media storm regarding such behavior and its consequences. The catalyst for this was the tragic suicide of the youngest person in Iceland to ever consider this act the only option. The boy was eleven, and his life had been made hell because of bullying. He hanged himself in his room.

Both this news and the discussion that followed filled me with great sadness. But the more I read the angrier I became. And as a crime writer, anger is often a good source for ideas. What fills you with anger might just be something that would lead someone a bit more unhinged to kill. I must emphasize that the tradeoff, a young child's life for an idea for a book, bear no comparison. I would gladly have rubbished the idea if life could rewind and save this child. But as this is not an option, instead I wrote in the hope of drawing more attention to the topic by whittling out a compelling mystery with bullying at its core.

When I was growing up, the Icelandic word for bullying (einelti) did not exist, or, if it did, it was confined to dictionaries and was never used. What we today recognize as bullying was called "teasing" (stríðni) or just "kids being kids". I am unsure of when the term bullying became a part of our everyday language. As far as I can see, the word first appeared in laws and regulations regarding safety in the workplace just after the turn of the millennium. As legislature takes time to write and approve, I would think it safe to bet that the word came into its own in the late 90s.

While the late 20th century gave us the addition of an appropriate term to the language, and thereby acknowledged the existence of the problem, the birth of social media and other internet platforms aimed at portraying user content helped us understand the full implications. With it, bullying was provided a steroid injection that took away the physical boundaries that had so far limited its spread of venom. Yes, in the past, there was graffiti on the occasional wall, stating that this girl or that boy was a wimp, loser, pervert or some other type of vile name-calling. But in most part bullying was limited to the physical presence of the bully and the bullying victim in the same location. The bully would insult, harass or harm the victim and those in close vicinity would witness the torture. Providing that the bully was not a close family member the victim could count on a safe haven at home or in places where their paths were unlikely to cross. The schoolyard was without a doubt the top spot for such harassment as well as school hallways.

Today bullying knows no such boundaries. Bullies can go about their disgusting business wherever they are, as long as they have an internet connection. They do not need to be in the presence of their victim. Bullies now spew their repulsive poison onto the internet, knowing it will find not only an audience but also its way home. Bullies can hound their victims all the way into their bedroom and no place is safe. The outreach has also multiplied with the aid of the internet, since witnessing the humiliation of a victim does not require actually being there when it happens. The whole world can take part or silently witness. Few who do make any attempt to stop the harassment or point out how atrocious this behavior is. The biggest deterrent is probably fear of being next, seeing the spearheads pointed in your direction. In all of human history there has never been an excess of heroes. Today is no exception. Heroes are unfortunately few and far between.

Lastly, the internet has completely severed the small amount of empathy that might have held the bully back. There is no longer eye contact between the bully and the victim. Children (and adults) are much more likely to write completely disgusting and horrible things on an impersonal keyboard than they would say face to face to an actual person.

And so, by merging with the limitless opportunities of social interaction via the internet, bullying has found a match made in hell. The pairing is as vile and cruel as it gets.

So what can be done? Nothing?

Of course not. One of the more obvious actions would be for the internet platforms involved to man up and take some responsibility. Put some effort into removing such content and banning the users or the IP numbers associated with such postings. I am sure the most hardened bullies would find a way to get around this but at least it would make their loathsome actions more difficult and exasperating. It would furthermore act as a deterrent to those who choose to show following in the bully's ugly wake. The urge to be nasty would probably be subdued by administrative details.

Depending on the legal system, another way to tackle bullying is to lawyer-up. Sue the bully for malicious damage. The damage is easily quantifiable—loss of work for the parents that need to go pick up their crying child from school, falling grades that will impact the child's future opportunities of employment and salary, cost of counselling and any damaged belongings that might have borne the brunt of the violence. Providing proof of the actual bullying actions is also relatively easy if there is cyberbullying involved. Electronic traces are not hard to identify. Truthfully, it will be an uphill battle. But it is sure to get the attention of the bully's parents that are likely to finally do something to rein in their little monster. Because after all, who bear the final responsibility for their child's upbringing? The parents.

Lots more could also be done when it comes to focusing on the bully, not the victim. Forget about asking the bullied child to change or become invisible. Nothing a child does, says, looks like, enjoys or believes in, gives other kids the right to attack. Far from it. But the urge to bully does not come from a good place, and the most effective counseling might be that which is given to the bully, not the victim. Bullying is anti-social behavior, and given time, the bully is a hell of a lot more likely to become a dangerous grown up than a kid that acts civilized and kindly. Is that not something that should be nipped in the bud if at all possible?

Another strategy, and the one most relevant to this audience, is childhood reading. Encouraging children to read is known to increase empathy by placing the reader in the shoes of varying characters and into situations that they might never be in otherwise. Reading does this in a manner that other forms of entertainment cannot. The reader enters the thoughts of the characters and experiences, as if in his or her own skin, the consequences of varying actions. You feel for those that are subject to injustice and are thus less likely to cause injustice yourself. Computer games and films are not able to do this. The viewer or gamer is always an onlooker. But the more you read, the more you understand others. The more you understand others, the more you feel for those who face adversity, racism, marginalization or any other form of injustice, big or small. The more you read, better a person you become.

An empathetic child will not bully. Avid readers are not bullies.

But as this is published on a reader site, this does of course mean that I have been typing out my thoughts on bullying for the abyss. You, dear reader, are not a bully—of this I am sure.

When writing The Absolution, seething with anger, I did not have to make up the disgusting comments attributed to the bullies of the book. I picked them up from various Icelandic articles about online bullying in which victims laid bare the abuse they were subject to through social media. When done, I thought about dedicating the book to bullies; to say something akin to: This book is for all bullies out there. Watch out. You are playing with fire mofo. But as I said above, bullies are not readers. They would never see the dedication. So I skipped it. I am still not sure if I regret it or not.

Viewpoint 2

> *"Even the most reticent person offline can turn a potential bully online. Further, anonymity allows them to unleash the monster in them towards strangers and friends alike."*

In India, Cyberbullying Increased During the Pandemic

Ullekh NP

This viewpoint considers cyberbullying in India after the outbreak of COVID-19, when the pandemic forced people to isolate. According to surveys, this situation led to a stunning rise in cyberbullying. Types of cyberbullying identified include stalking, derogatory comments, leaking pictures or videos, and harassment. Many victims face more than one of these tactics. Victims are urged to take action against their harassers, as cyberbullies, like all bullies, feel most powerful when their victims are weak and pose no threat to them. Ullekh NP is an author, journalist and political commentator based in New Delhi.

As you read, consider the following questions:

1. What are some of the factors that increased cyberbullying during the pandemic?
2. According to the NMIMS study, what effect did cyberbullying have on victims?
3. Why are some Indian cyberspaces "hubs" of bullying?

"Cruelty of the Mysterious Man," by Ullekh NP, Open Media Network, October 16, 2020. Reprinted by permission.

Ratan Tata, Chairman, Tata Trusts, and chairman emeritus, Tata Sons, is on Instagram, the Facebook-owned social networking service where "stories" are essentially photos and videos. With three million followers, the former business tycoon has till October 14th shared only as low as 32 "stories" and that includes photos of him as a schoolkid in America in 1955 and one with his late dog Tito, among others. By his own admission, his familiarity with the social networking space isn't deep, yet he sensed that people were pulling down each other online, which is also known as bullying. That prompted him to appeal to bullies sometime in June: "This year has been full of challenges for everyone, on some level or the other. I see the online community being hurtful to each other, bringing each other down, harshly and with quick judgments." Tata has been sharp at diagnosing the malaise called bullying although he said his presence online was "limited."

Mumbai-based researchers who have been analysing cyberbullying before and during Covid-19 find their results confirming Tata's worst fears: that it is in the most challenging times in recent history—lockdown—that bullies have unleashed their fury over others on social networking sites and messaging platforms.

Actor and filmmaker Pooja Bhatt even received death threats on Instagram, forcing her to make her account private and come out with tweets about her ordeal. "People threatening violence/ hurling abuse, suggesting you die seems to have become a norm on @instagram when reported, #Instagram mostly responds saying that the conduct does not go against their guidelines & suggests you block them. #Twitter has far better standards/guidelines," Bhatt wrote. "What's even worse is that most of the abuse and messages screaming 'Go die' or 'why don't you kill yourself' come from women or at least people pretending to be women—one can't really tell with @instagram anymore. Get your act together @ instagram cyberbullying is a crime," she wrote from her verified Twitter handle.

If you thought such attacks had only to do with the furor and anger, manufactured or otherwise, over the death of young actor

Sushant Singh Rajput whose case undoubtedly acquired political and provincial colours, the study, mentioned earlier and conducted by a team of enthusiastic researchers at the Narsee Monjee Institute of Management Studies (NMIMS), which was published in the Elsevier peer-reviewed publication in late September, busts all such myths. *Open* has followed this trauma-inducing trend of cyberbullying that involves hacking, verbal abuse and nuanced body shaming, besides others, for long. But the situation, as studies and numbers from agencies suggest, is hurtling out of control with more people entering the online space to entertain themselves and to seek the pleasures of offline platforms online thanks to the lockdown.

"Owing to the Covid-19-induced lockdown in India, most people's internet activity surged, leading to an expected increase in the rate of cybercrimes. This research focuses on analysing whether the factors significant in cyber-bullying susceptibility changed with the lockdown," announces the Elsevier paper titled "Has the COVID-19 pandemic affected the susceptibility to cyberbullying in India?" The study, which surveyed 256 students before the pandemic in October 2019 and 118 students during the lockdown in June 2020, is authored by Ojasvi Jain, Muskan Gupta, Sidh Satam and Siba Panda.

Jain, who is a BTech student of data science at the institute, told Open that the team had collected data on cyberbullying ahead of the pandemic and after Covid struck, decided to do another survey to make a comparative analysis. The results were shocking in that it showed a rapid rise in bullying on a range of factors, including age and other demographic variables.

This paper argues why the number of cases of cyberbullying has grown faster than usual during the lockdown. It says, "New factors emerged such as Instagram as a preferred social media platform along with the number of games and gaming chat platforms preferred by respondents. Apart from these, even demographics of the respondents such as their age and sexual orientation were found significant during the COVID-19 pandemic, which were not significant before. The emergence of these new factors and their degree of significance, depicts a change in cyberbullying susceptibility and can provide for the basis of study for future researchers."

According to the NMIMS study, the most prominent form of cyberbullying is stalking (71.21 per cent) followed by posting derogatory comments (64.39 per cent), leaking pictures/videos online (41.67 per cent) and harassing (21.97 per cent). All this also signifies that most individuals have faced more than one type of cyberbullying, the authors reason.

The majority of the victims surveyed for this study said that they were not negatively impacted by the act (37.88 per cent) whereas 30.30 per cent said they were negatively impacted. Unfortunately, although the Government has advertised it many times that complaints should be promptly made on www.cybercrime.gov.in, the study found that the severest reaction

Another Side Effect of the Pandemic

With schools closed and events canceled to protect our families from the spread of COVID-19, an increased amount of time online presents another risk to children—cyberbullying. Particularly for children with epilepsy, cyberbullying can perpetuate negative stigmas that are harmful to a child's happiness and sense of security.

A child with special health needs or chronic illness is more likely to be bullied because they are often "othered" by their peers. However, as a parent or guardian, there are steps you can take to protect your child from cyberbullying.

When a child is bullied, it may not be easy for them to talk about it. Make sure your child knows that they can come to you with any issues. Building a healthy support system of family and friends is also essential! Your child needs to know there is someone right by their side, whether it's when they have a seizure or when someone is bullying them online.

by the victims was only reporting and blocking perpetrators on social media platforms. In fact, one should not run into a conclusion that such online platforms are any less concerned about such bullying. They have also advertised aggressively, asking the victims to report bullies. But cyber analysts contend that they could do more than asking them to report. "In fact, they just ask you to block the malefactor," a Delhi-based senior government official said.

The Mumbai study concludes that the victims mostly blocked their bullies on social media platforms (39.39 per cent of the respondents did so), many others ignored them (29.55 per cent). "Merely 4.55 per cent of the victims took legal action against the bully by reporting them to the concerned government authorities," the report says. As in the case of sexual assault offline, a majority of the attackers were known to the victims here too. In 68.18 per cent of the cases, the perpetrator was known to the victim, and

> Empower your child to protect themselves online by teaching them basic online etiquette. When your child is cyberbullied, the simplest and most straightforward solution is to block or report the person. You can teach your child how to do this themselves.
>
> Also, it's crucial to teach your child NOT to engage with cyberbullies or online trolls. Cyberbullies and online trolls are trying to bate you into responding. By not engaging, you are taking away their power.
>
> With young children, you should try to limit their unsupervised time online. When this isn't possible, creating a separate profile with limited privileges is a simple solution. Limiting privileges is becoming easier for parents with sites like YouTube requiring content creators to set an intended age group for every video they upload.
>
> **"The Prevalence of Cyberbullying During the Pandemic," Epilepsy Foundation Central & South Texas.**

the authors contend that familiarity could be behind the gross underreporting of cases.

In some cases, victims treat the bitter experience as par for the course. "We grin and bear it because it is seen as an unpardonable offence if we complain even to school authorities about someone hacking into our social media sites, especially Instagram," says a former female student of Delhi Public School, RK Puram. In fact, in her book, *Stoned, Shamed, Depressed: An Explosive Account of the Secret Lives of India's Teens*, author Jyotsna Mohan Bhargava writes about how teens take pride in hacking somebody else's account to fit in while the victim seems to derive a certain pleasure in the fact that her account was hacked into. She describes it as a badge of honour for some people. Bhargava writes, "Many hacking victims dismiss it as a rite of passage in school—you aren't relevant if your account hasn't been hacked at least once."

Even those who make such posturing and many others go through unexplainable trauma and long-term psychological consequences. The Omerta-kind of code that insists only the faint-hearted approach authorities, drive many of them to psychiatrists and counsellors. "I have seen many teens under counselling commit suicide and many others coming back from suicide attempts struggle to get back to being normal. It is a constant struggle and the stories are mostly untold and suppressed in the name of everything from family honour to ensure that these experiences don't impinge on their lives in the future, since India is a country where there are stigmas attached to everything from mental illness to meeting shrinks," says a reputed psychologist who spoke on condition of anonymity so as not to embarrass her patients.

The NMIMS study, unsurprisingly, throws up an interesting result as regards the action against the perpetrator. There is not much change in pre and post-Covid periods despite the rise in cases in the latter period. The study makes some recommendations: "Various stakeholders such as students, parents, government authorities, psychology experts, and researchers can leverage these findings to spread more awareness about the impacts of cyberbullying to curtail the number of cases and encourage the victims to report these cases to proper authorities. Further studies from the bully's perspective can also be conducted to get more information on the various reasons behind cyberbullying." The paper adds, "Apart from this, studies can focus on the causal relations between the various significant factors. Statistical post-hoc tests can be conducted to delve deeper into these causal relations. Various interaction effects can also be considered to get a better understanding of the matter and create a profile for an individual who is more susceptible to cyberbullying and understand its impact on different demographic groups."

In some cases of cyberbullying, as police confirm, victims find out about being trashed online only after months or, maybe, years. For instance, Kriti, who doesn't want to use her surname and lives in Gurugram, noticed that she couldn't log on to her Facebook account for two days, but she saw nothing wrong with it: she thought it was some technical glitch. In reality, what happened was that her Facebook (FB) account was hacked and private and dirty messages were sent to one of her FB friends whom she was not in touch with for long.

Two days later, she used her mobile phone number and other "clues" to create a new password and joined FB. Life was normal until she was contacted by her FB friend much later with the screenshots of the raunchy texts he had received from her detailing some fictitious sexual exploits of hers in crass language. Her messages were immediately deleted by the person who hacked into her FB account, so she herself could not view them. "Since my old friend understood that it could not be me, he warned me to be careful about hacking, but I never complained to anyone after that," says this young lady who is a fresh graduate. "Such attitude is wrong," says a Delhi Police officer who has probed many cybercrime cases involving young people. "These days, thanks to Covid, even older people end up as victims of cyberbullying because they are also online," he points out. Various police officers *Open* spoke to across states and Union Territories also shared the view that the

"Covid season" saw a sharp increase in cyberattacks, including stalking and abusive comments online.

Mumbai-based Nirali Bhatia, a cyber psychologist and psychotherapist, who is also the founder of Cyber BAAP, which helps victims of cyberbullying, explains to Open why bullies who have recently surfaced online are unlikely to disappear once the Covid-19 blues end.

"During lockdown, cyberspace has been our only getaway. Be it for communication, socialising, work, education or entertainment. So, certainly during this period, there has been a huge hike in the number of people going online across all age groups," she affirms and goes on to add that the tricky thing about cyberspace is that it is designed to be addictive. "Nonstop, unlimited information is pushed to us. It is available 24×7 and offers instant gratification and wide popularity." That is why she says most often new entrants into online platforms are hooked forever.

Bhatia concedes that in the past five months she has received more than 2,500 cases of cyberbullying and harassment on her anti-cyberbullying portal www.cyberbaap.org, which is much higher than before. "Maximum bullying cases amongst the youth are on Instagram, while for those over 25 years of age, it is either dating sites, WhatsApp or Facebook. Victims under the age of 13 have reported bullying on gaming chat rooms and portals like Discord," she states.

Bullies thrive on anonymity offered by certain platforms and hence some spaces are hubs of bullying, she confirms, emphasising that such social media and online gaming platforms have no methods to validate users. "Another big reason is these platforms have no regulations for Indian regional languages and bullies are taking advantage of it. These days, we have maximum cases where hurtful comments or threats are made in regional languages, which when reported, do not meet guidelines of bullying on these social media platforms," adds Bhatia. Twitter abounds in such complaints, most recently by the co-founder of Alt News, a fact-checking website, who put up a screenshot this week of Twitter's response to a malicious Hindi tweet he had reported, saying it did not violate Twitter norms, though Hindi speakers would understand the threat behind it.

As an expert who meets or e-meets a large number of victims of cyberbullying, Bhatia says such experiences can lead to severe psychological conditions such as depression, anxiety and suicidal tendencies. "We want no victim to ever feel there is no hope or no help available. On our portal, we have made a provision for the victims to report to us so that we can counsel and guide them to deal with the incident, hand-hold them in reporting this to the police, offer investigations service and, lastly, we also conduct cyber safety awareness workshops," Bhatia tells *Open*. She encourages victims to report cyberbullying on www.cybercrime.gov.in before they approach her.

Even the most reticent person offline can turn a potential bully online. Further, anonymity allows them to unleash the monster in them towards strangers and friends alike. The lockdown has seen more people becoming bullies online. They have tasted blood and the only way to stop them is extensive reporting of all kinds of cyberattacks to instill in them the fear of punishment. After all, bullies mostly thrive when they feel their victims are weak.

Viewpoint 3

> *"As long as policy-makers and stakeholders see [cyberbullying] as primarily an e-safety problem, we will have difficulties finding adequate solutions."*

Social Media Companies Have the Wrong Approach to Cyberbullying

Kate Gilchrist

In this interview with Tijana Milosevic, a researcher at Dublin City University's Anti-Bullying Centre and author of Protecting Children Online? Cyberbullying Policies of Social Media Companies, *Kate Gilcrest and Milosevic discuss the role of social media companies in protecting children and teens from cyberbullying. Milosevic finds little evidence that efforts by these companies to protect youth are effective and repeatedly calls for social media companies to gain insights from young people in order to better protect them and serve their needs. Kate Gilchrist, Ph. D., works in the Department of Media and Communications at the London School of Economics and is a Lecturer at University College London.*

"How Are Social Media Companies Protecting Children Online? Evaluating Anti-Cyberbullying," by Kate Gilchrist, London School of Economics, August 22, 2018. https://blogs.lse.ac.uk/parenting4digitalfuture/2018/08/22/protecting-children-online/.

As you read, consider the following questions:

1. What are some of Milosevic's primary findings from her study of cyberbullying?
2. Why does she believe the key issue is not e-safety but human dignity?
3. Why does she feel that there needs to be a de-emphasis on punitive measures in dealing with cyberbullies?

There have been a number of recent initiatives that hold the internet industry to account for online bullying—but how effective have they been? We interview Tijana Milosevic about her new book *Protecting Children Online? Cyberbullying Policies of Social Media Companies*, which is a timely examination of how social media platforms are tackling the problem of harassment of children online. Here Tijana recommends that the child should be centred in the evaluation of such initiatives and that dignity education could be part of the solution. Tijana is a postdoctoral researcher at the University of Oslo focusing on social media policies, internet governance, and digital media use among children and youth.

Congratulations on the publication of your book. Can you tell us how you came to choose this topic, and why you think it is important?

The starting point for *Protecting Children Online? Cyberbullying Policies of Social Media Companies* was realising that there was insufficient information about the measures that social media companies were taking to address the problem of cyberbullying of children and teens. This was strange, given that researchers and stakeholders recognised the increasing importance of social media platforms in young people's lives and the ongoing debates on whether social media companies should be regulated as online intermediaries or as publishers.

I wanted to find out what social media companies were doing to address cyberbullying; what could be known about the effectiveness of their efforts; how effective regulation had been; and how debates on intermediary liability evolved in the aftermath of high-profile cyberbullying cases—those that gathered significant public attention because they were said to have been, in some way, related to child suicides.

When I refer to "effectiveness" and "evidence of effectiveness" I mean available information on whether children and teens are using social media companies' tools against bullying (e.g. blocking, reporting, information provided in Safety Centres etc.) and whether the tools are actually helping them resolve bullying incidents. For instance, if a child uses a reporting tool to flag an alleged bullying case to the company, does the company respond and does it respond in due time? If it responds, does the bullying content get taken down or is some other action taken? Or is the content allowed to remain on the platform? Do content take-down, and other mechanisms that companies have, actually help young people in resolving such conflicts? If the company is leveraging some form of what could be characterised as machine learning or artificial intelligence in addressing the problem, how is this being done? And what evidence does the company provide that these tools are effective in helping it identify bullying cases and respond to them in a timely manner?

The book is based on several years of research—can you tell us how you went about your research, and your main findings?

I conducted a qualitative analysis of 14 social media companies' corporate documents and statements and carried out interviews with several of their representatives. I also interviewed members of non-governmental organisations or charities that work with social media companies, as well as non-affiliated e-safety experts; and finally I analysed public debates surrounding high-profile cyberbullying incidents. I also compared the different approaches taken in the US and European contexts. The main findings were:

- There was a limited amount of evidence about the effectiveness of companies' anti-bullying enforcement mechanisms.
- There was even less evidence on whether these mechanisms were effective from the perspective of children, as few studies looked directly at children's experiences of such mechanisms.
- More established social media companies put more effort into developing their anti-bullying enforcement mechanisms but also tended to ensure their efforts were more visible; this can sometimes obscure the fact that palpable evidence of effectiveness is limited. At one point, companies were moving towards tools for users to resolve conflicts amongst themselves rather than only reporting to companies' moderators; this was said to allow for more effective resolutions but also appeared to shift responsibility away from the companies.
- Where laws aimed at addressing cyberbullying among youth had been proposed or passed it was difficult to demonstrate that such laws were effective, while some laws had/would have negative implications for freedom of speech and privacy of adults.
- In Europe the European Commission has played a significant role in bringing companies together in a coordinated effort, to create various self-regulatory processes. In the US, such a systematic effort has largely been missing.

Why do you think bullying has become such a problem in the digital age? Does it merit a particular societal response or would it be more efficient to try and reduce risk through one big internet safety strategy?

I do not think that cyberbullying is primarily an e-safety problem but one of human dignity and as long as policy-makers and stakeholders see it as primarily an e-safety problem, we will have difficulties finding adequate solutions. I think there should be mechanisms in place that allow children (and adults) to control abusive content. But by focusing on content take-down or other forms of conflict resolution in any specific incident (which I do not deny are extremely important), we forget that cyberbullying tends to be a relational problem; one that is sustained through what I see as a pervasive culture of "one-upmanship".

Yes, we have cases of trolling and harassment where a number of individuals that the victim may not know harass the individual, where thinking about the problem in terms of safety could lead

Has Cyberbullying Been Exaggerated?

Cyberbullying continues to be the topic du jour, especially for school administrators and legislators, both of which feel something needs to be done, even if they both have nothing in the form of hard data showing the threat matches the perception.

The result is bad policies and worse laws aimed at fighting an exaggerated problem. How exaggerated is it? Well, that depends on who you ask.... [But] the numbers tend to rise if there's a product or service in play.

I got a call recently from a woman who works for a company that makes an app designed to "keep kids safe" by enabling parents to monitor their texts and social media activities. The pitch included some dire statistics such as "70 percent of kids are cyberbullied" and—like other companies that make parental-control software—I was also told that it helps protect kids from strangers who would do them harm.

Actual studies point to much lower numbers, although there's no solid consensus.

The National Center for Educational Statistics reports that 6 percent of students in grades 6-12 experienced cyberbullying. The Centers for Disease Control found in 2011 that 16.2 percent of students had been bullied via email, chat rooms, instant messaging, websites or to adequate solutions. But many cases are about identity-related issues where children know each other well—too well. When it comes to girls, for example, who is prettier, better dressed—these are often at the heart of bullying conflicts and drama. Western countries, as well as the so-called transitional countries, are immersed in a neoliberal culture where we teach children to draw self-worth from external insignia of success—looks, money, grades, etc.

Combating cyberbullying lies in finding effective ways to teach young people and adults alike that everyone has dignity regardless of these external insignia and that one's inherent worth

texting—compared to 20.1 percent who had been bullied on school property (traditional bullying)—during the 12 months prior to the survey. The Cyberbullying Research Center reports that "on average, about 24 percent of the students who have been a part of our last six studies have said they have been the victim of cyberbullying at some point in their lifetime."

Dan Olweus, who the editor of the European Journal of Development Psychology referred to as the "father of bullying research" wrote a 2012 article for that journal where he said that "claims about cyberbullying made in the media and elsewhere are greatly exaggerated and have little empirical scientific support." Based on a three-year survey of more than 440,000 U.S. children (between 3rd and 12th grade), 4.5 percent of kids had been cyberbullied compared to 17.6 percent from that same sample who had experienced traditional bullying. An even more interesting statistic from that study is that only 2.8 percent of kids had bullied others.

Because cyberbullying isn't precisely defined, variations are to be expected. But even the most expansive definitions fail to return the scary numbers quoted by those pushing software, policies and legislation.

"The Exaggeration of the Cyberbullying Problem Is Harming Anti-Bullying Efforts," by Tim Cushing, Techdirt, October 11, 2013.

is not based on being better than the next person but on fulfilling one's full, unique potential. Understanding this, in my view, would obviate humiliation. I think that dignity education can be taught under digital citizenship education but it will take a lot of thinking and planning as to how such education should be designed and implemented for it to be effective.

As I have elaborated previously here, citing some of my interviewees, it is important to have a clear understanding of what digital citizenship education is for it to be more than a re-branded term for e-safety education. Once it is clearly defined and operationalised, evaluating the effectiveness of such education should be undertaken, see here. In my view, the term runs the danger of becoming a catch-all phrase or a buzzword: a popular term in policy circles that is used to signal a positive change. We need to ensure that concrete steps are attached to it and that their effectiveness can be evaluated.

What are the lessons of your work for current regulatory debates? What do you think industry—and regulators—should do differently?

De-focusing on regulation and focusing instead on how we can evaluate companies' efforts from the perspective of children would allow us to move beyond the usual mantras reinforced by insufficiently researched laws or hasty proposals for regulation that have negative effects on civil liberties—mantras such as "traditional regulation stifles innovation" or "laws are too slow to adapt to fast-paced technological change".

Therefore, rather than focusing on hasty proposals for new pieces of legislation, policy-makers should conduct regular independent evaluation of the effectiveness of various companies' anti-bullying enforcement mechanisms, so that we understand the gaps and—more importantly—where children see the gaps.

How could civil society (child welfare organisations, academic researchers, parent organisations etc.) be more effective in promoting children's rights in digital environments?

Involving children in the evaluation process is the first step. It is also extremely important for companies that work with non-governmental organizations or e-safety experts to be more transparent and allow third parties to talk about their efforts and evaluate them more openly and critically. A common practice that I found in my research was that large companies would require these third parties to sign non-disclosure agreements which could then limit what they could talk about with researchers. I think that transparency is important when it comes to allowing researchers who do not work "in-house" to have access to the relevant data. National and international governance bodies need to provide more funding for these third parties so that they do not have to be dependent on companies.

To conclude, I think that a lot of the debate around cyberbullying, including the discussion on regulating social media companies, has overly emphasised punitive measures. This blame-gaming discourse tends to be reductionist with respect to the complexity of cyberbullying as a phenomenon. I wonder if, when thinking about regulation, a more effective approach would be to focus on enabling rather than merely punitive measures, such as: requiring companies to assist in funding school-based educational measures; funding support for parents and helpline services; funding psychological and counseling services for children and families, which are normally underfunded.

Viewpoint 4

"Social media isn't just mirroring conflicts happening in schools and on streets—it's intensifying and triggering new conflicts."

Social Media Can Turn Online Arguments Between Teens into Real-World Violence

Caitlin Elsaesser

In the following viewpoint Caitlin Elsaesser argues that social media has the power to incite violence among teens. The author's research found that social media can trigger offline violence, particularly among young people who live in disenfranchised urban neighborhoods, and that features such as comments, live streaming, and video sharing can escalate conflicts to real world physical fights. Avoiding such conflict requires active de-escalation tactics, which prove difficult because of influences like peer pressure. Caitlin Elsaesser is Assistant Professor of Social Work at the University of Connecticut.

As you read, consider the following questions:

1. How has the author studied the subject matter and obtained findings?
2. How can live streaming escalate a conflict?
3. When is the bystander intervention strategy most effective?

"How Social Media Turns Online Arguments Between Teens into Real-World Violence," by Caitlin Elsaesser, The Conversation, April 5, 2021, https://theconversation.com/how-social-media-turns-online-arguments-between-teens-into-real-world-violence-155613.

The deadly insurrection at the U.S. Capitol in January exposed the power of social media to influence real-world behavior and incite violence. But many adolescents, who spend more time on social media than all other age groups, have known this for years.

"On social media, when you argue, something so small can turn into something so big so fast," said Justin, a 17-year-old living in Hartford, Connecticut, during one of my research focus groups. (The participants' names have been changed in this article to protect their identities.)

For the last three years, I have studied how and why social media triggers and accelerates offline violence. In my research, conducted in partnership with Hartford-based peace initiative COMPASS Youth Collaborative, we interviewed dozens of young people aged 12-19 in 2018. Their responses made clear that social media is not a neutral communication platform.

In other words, social media isn't just mirroring conflicts happening in schools and on streets—it's intensifying and triggering new conflicts. And for young people who live in disenfranchised urban neighborhoods, where firearms can be readily available, this dynamic can be deadly.

Internet Banging

It can result in a phenomenon that researchers at Columbia University have coined "internet banging." Distinct from cyberbullying, internet banging involves taunts, disses and arguments on social media between people in rival crews, cliques or gangs. These exchanges can include comments, images and videos that lead to physical fights, shootings and, in the worst cases, death.

It is estimated that the typical U.S. teen uses screen media more than seven hours daily, with the average teenager daily using three different forms of social media. Films such as "The Social Dilemma" underscore that social media companies create addictive platforms by design, using features such as unlimited scrolling and push notifications to keep users endlessly engaged.

According to the young people we interviewed, four social media features in particular escalate conflicts: comments, livestreaming, picture/video sharing and tagging.

Comments and Livestreams

The feature most frequently implicated in social media conflicts, according to our research with adolescents, was comments. Roughly 80% of the incidents they described involved comments, which allow social media users to respond publicly to content posted by others.

Taylor, 17, described how comments allow people outside her friend group to "hype up" online conflicts: "On Facebook if I have an argument, it would be mostly the outsiders that'll be hypin' us up … 'Cause the argument could have been done, but you got outsiders being like, 'Oh, she gonna beat you up.'"

Meanwhile, livestreaming can quickly attract a large audience to watch conflict unfold in real time. Nearly a quarter of focus group participants implicated Facebook Live, for example, as a feature that escalates conflict.

Brianna, 17, shared an example in which her cousin told another girl to come to her house to fight on Facebook Live. "But mind you, if you got like 5,000 friends on Facebook, half of them watching … And most of them live probably in the area you live in. You got some people that'll be like, 'Oh, don't fight.' But in the majority, everybody would be like, 'Oh, yeah, fight.'"

She went on to describe how three Facebook "friends" who were watching the livestream pulled up in cars in front of the house with cameras, ready to record and then post any fight.

Strategies to Stop Violence

Adolescents tend to define themselves through peer groups and are highly attuned to slights to their reputation. This makes it difficult to resolve social media conflicts peacefully. But the young people we spoke with are highly aware of how social media shapes the nature and intensity of conflicts.

A key finding of our work is that young people often try to avoid violence resulting from social media. Those in our study discussed four approaches to do so: avoidance, deescalation, reaching out for help and bystander intervention.

Avoidance involves exercising self-control to avoid conflict in the first place. As 17-year-old Diamond explained, "If I'm scrolling and I see something and I feel like I got to comment, I'll go [to] comment and I'll be like, 'Hold up, wait, no.' And I just start deleting it and tell myself … 'No, mind my business.'"

Reaching out for support involves turning to peers, family or teachers for help. "When I see conflict, I screenshot it and send it to my friends in our group chat and laugh about it," said Brianna, 16. But there's a risk in this strategy, Brianna noted: "You could screenshot something on Snapchat, and it'll tell the person that you screenshot it and they'll be like, 'Why are you screenshotting my stuff?'"

The deescalation strategy involves attempts by those involved to slow down a social media conflict as it happens. However, participants could not recount an example of this strategy working, given the intense pressure they experience from social media comments to protect one's reputation.

They emphasized the bystander intervention strategy was most effective offline, away from the presence of an online audience. A friend might start a conversation offline with an involved friend to help strategize how to avoid future violence. Intervening online is often risky, according to participants, because the intervener can become a new target, ultimately making the conflict even bigger.

Peer Pressure Goes Viral

Young people are all too aware that the number of comments a post garners, or how many people are watching a livestream, can make it extremely difficult to pull out of a conflict once it starts.

Jasmine, a 15-year-old, shared, "On Facebook, there be so many comments, so many shares and I feel like the other person would feel like they would be a punk if they didn't step, so they step even though they probably, deep down, really don't want to step."

There is a growing consensus across both major U.S. political parties that the large technology companies behind social media apps need to be more tightly regulated. Much of the concern has focused on the dangers of unregulated free speech.

But from the vantage point of the adolescents we spoke with in Hartford, conflict that occurs on social media is also a public health threat. They described multiple experiences of going online without the intention to fight, and getting pulled into an online conflict that ended up in gun violence. Many young people are improvising strategies to avoid social media conflict. I believe parents, teachers, policymakers and social media engineers ought to listen closely to what they are saying.

Periodical and Internet Sources Bibliography

The following articles have been selected to supplement the diverse views presented in this chapter.

Mona Abboud, "OPINION: Social media is distorting our opinions." *The Red & Black*. June 25, 2021. https://www.redandblack.com/opinion/opinion-social-media-is-distorting-our-opinions/article_7b3e602c-d556-11eb-84cd-f7bfc821d8bc.html.

Sam Cook, "Cyberbullying facts and statistics for 2018 – 2022," Comparitech. January 29, 2022. https://www.comparitech.com/internet-providers/cyberbullying-statistics/.

Arlin Cuncic, "The Psychology of Cyberbullying," Very Well Mind. February 19, 2022. https://www.verywellmind.com/the-psychology-of-cyberbullying-5086615.

Ogi Djuraskovic, "Cyberbullying Statistics, Facts, and Trends (2022) with Charts," First Site Guide. https://firstsiteguide.com/cyberbullying-stats/.

Christo Petrov, "50 Alarming Cyberbullying Statistics for 2022," *Techjury*. March 14, 2022. https://techjury.net/blog/cyberbullying-statistics/.

Peter Suciu, "Cyberbullying Remains Rampant on Social Media," *Forbes*, September 29, 2021. https://www.forbes.com/sites/petersuciu/2021/09/29/cyberbullying-remains-rampant-on-social-media/

Calli Tzani, John Synnott, and Maria Ioannou, "Cyberbullying Among Teens: Our Research Shows Online Abuse and School Bullying Are Often Linked," The Conversation, October 6, 2021. https://theconversation.com/cyberbullying-among-teens-our-research-shows-online-abuse-and-school-bullying-are-often-linked-119442

Beau Yarbrough, "Cyberbullying Victims Are More Likely to Suffer from Depression. Here's How to Spot It and Stop It," The Mercury News, March 24, 2022. https://www.sbsun.com/2022/03/23/how-parents-and-teachers-can-detect-and-respond-to-cyberbullying-of-kids/

OPPOSING VIEWPOINTS® SERIES

Chapter 4

Is Teen Privacy at Risk on Social Media?

Chapter Preface

Could the single biggest threat to the online privacy of teens be coming from inside their own houses? Is it their own parents who knowingly or unwittingly post sensitive information about their children for their friends, and perhaps strangers, to see? Such seems to be the case in the early 21st century. As adults followed their children in flocking to social media sites such as Facebook, they began to share their lives. The old expression, "keeping up with the Joneses," has migrated online. In the past one needed a nice house, car, and lifestyle to suggest to their neighbors that they were affluent. Now, posts about family vacations, children's endeavors on the ball fields and in classrooms, and other points of family pride provide proof that one is living the American Dream.

The term "sharenting" was apparently coined in 2010 and is attributed to *The Wall Street Journal*. It describes parents who proudly post information, not about themselves, but about their children, online. In her book *Sharenthood*, professor Leah Plunkett of the University of New Hampshire offers a more comprehensive definition: sharenting "refers to a parent, teacher, or other adult caregiver who publishes, transmits, stores, or engages in other activities involving private information about a child in her or his care via digital channels."

Sharenting might seem to be a harmless diversion, just a parent taking pride in the exploits of his or her children. But, as with much activity on the world wide web, there is a darker side. Big tech collects information shared online, uses it to target consumers, and more. Plunkett offers one example of how such collections begin from the earliest age:

> Facebook can add your post about toilet training dilemmas as a data point to its own information about you, as well as whatever information it is sharing with third parties. Barbie, Elmo, new nanny: it's all data. The question isn't "who might be interested in this kind of dossier on kids?" but "Who wouldn't be?"

"Is this stuff happening already?" Plunkett asks. "Yes, it is." In the world of big tech and big data, companies are collecting troves of information. One might argue that in this giant haystack of information, tidbits about a single child are a needle that may never be found. But we can't be so sure. Just as corporations can collect the data, they can sell it to those who can disaggregate the information and then target it.

Should parents therefore abandon Facebook, or, at least, stop posting every time their teen hits a shot on the basketball court or buys a pet rabbit? Given that this is unlikely to happen, the subtitle of Plunkett's book seems apropos: "Why We Should Think before We Talk about Our Kids Online."

The viewpoints in this chapter consider not only the practice of sharenting, but other behaviors that endanger teen privacy, as well as the dangers that crop up when teens are too transparent online.

Viewpoint 1

> "One-third of teens say they delete or restrict access to things they share on social media because they are concerned it could negatively impact them later in life."

Teens Share Their Lives Online

Monica Anderson and Jingjing Jiang

In this viewpoint, Monica Anderson and Jingjing Jiang discuss the results of a survey regarding social media habits. Teens share everything from their social lives, to dating, to opinions on various matters, to selfies. Teens tend to share their lives openly with others, and while some do block a variety of users from seeing their information, most do not curate their online activity. According to the survey, few teens consider the negative impact their posts might have and, consequently, do not attempt to minimize who might see them. Monica Anderson is associate director of research at Pew Research Center primarily studying internet and technology issues. Jingjing Jiang is a former Research Analyst at the Center.

As you read, consider the following questions:

1. What results did the survey find regarding the posting of selfies by teens?

"Teens and Their Experiences on Social Media," by Monica Anderson and Jingjing Jiang, Pew Research Center, November 28, 2018. Reprinted by permission.

2. How do the topics teens post about differ between age groups (younger vs. older teens)?
3. How does blocking others or "unfriending" differ between boys and girls?

Social media has given teens the ability to instantly connect with others and share their lives through photos, videos and status updates. Teens themselves describe these platforms as a key tool for connecting and maintaining relationships, being creative, and learning more about the world. But they also must contend with more negative aspects of social media use, such as drama and bullying or feeling pressure to present themselves in a certain way.

Teens Post About a Range of Topics on Social Media, with Posts About Their Accomplishments or Family Playing an Especially Prominent Role

When asked what topics they post about on social media, roughly half of teens say they post about their accomplishments on social media, while 44% say they post about their family. Around one-third (34%) say they share things related to their emotions and feelings on these sites, while 22% report posting about their dating life. Relatively few teens—around one-in-ten—say they share things related to their personal problems or their religious or political beliefs on social media.

There are some age and gender differences in the topics teens share on social media. Older teens are more likely than their younger counterparts to post about their romantic relationships: 26% of teens ages 15 to 17 say they post about their dating life on social media, compared with 16% of 13- to 14-year-olds.

Meanwhile, girls are more likely than boys to say they post about their family (53% vs. 36%), their emotions and feelings (40% vs. 29%) or their religious beliefs (14% vs. 7%). And older girls are especially likely to post about a variety of subjects—including their dating lives, their family, their emotions and their religious or political beliefs, compared with older boys or younger teens.

Selfies May Be Popular on Social Media, but Around Half of Teens Say They Rarely or Never Post These Images

Although the proliferation of smartphones has given teens the ability to constantly share different aspects of their lives, this survey finds that many teens regularly forego posting selfies, videos or other updates of their lives to social media.

Some 45% of teens say they often or sometimes post selfies on social media, with 16% saying they do this often. Similar shares of teens say they at least sometimes post things only their closest friends would understand (50%), updates on where they are or what they're doing (42%) or videos they've recorded (41%). A smaller share of teens report regularly posting things that they want to go viral (29%). Notably, in each instance close to half or more of teens say they rarely or never share these types of posts on social media.

There is some demographic variation in the types of content teens say they post to social media. Girls are much more likely than boys to post selfies: Six-in-ten girls say they often or sometimes do this, compared with 30% of boys. And while two-thirds of black teens and about half (51%) of Hispanic teens report regularly sharing selfies on social media, that share drops to 39% among white youth. Black teens are also much more likely than whites to say they at least sometimes post things they want to go viral (41% vs. 25%).

Teens Generally Believe Social Media Helps Deepen Friendships and Are More Likely to Equate Their Social Media Use with Positive Emotions—but This Positivity Is Far from Unanimous

A central conversation surrounding social media and young people is the impact these platforms may be having on the emotional well-being of teens. A majority of teens believe social media has had a positive impact on various aspects of their lives, the survey finds. Fully 81% of teens say social media makes them feel more connected to what's going on in their friends' lives, with 37% saying it makes them feel "a lot" more connected. Similarly, about seven-in-ten teens say these sites make them feel more in touch with their friends' feelings (69%), that they have people who will support them through tough times (68%), or that they have a place to show their creative side (71%).

But although sizable shares of teens encounter positive experiences on social media, some report encountering drama or feeling pressure to present themselves in a certain way. Some 45% of teens say they feel overwhelmed by all the drama on social media, while roughly four-in-ten say they feel pressure to only post content that makes them look good to others or that will get lots of comments or likes. Others believe social media has had a negative impact on their self-esteem: 26% of teens say these sites make them feel worse about their own life.

A False Sense of Security

Teens have never known a world without data sharing. But this familiarity offers a false sense of security. To puncture it, we need to simplify the complexities associated with online data and digital identity. How do social platforms gather and share data to personalize content, develop differentiated services and connect users? How does an intricate web of third-party data aggregators collect and share data to retarget online users?

Understanding the risk associated with readily available online information and the myriad ways someone might use it (or exploit it), is a complex, dynamic story. Talking about the potential damage to your credit score might not hit the mark for a 17-year-old. Even a discussion on how your social media profile might be perceived by employers and colleges might not have the desired impact for a generation that often seems to value openness over privacy.

Still, just 4% of teens indicate these platforms make them feel "a lot" worse about their life.

The survey also presented teens with four pairs of words and asked them to choose the sentiment that most closely matches how they feel when using social media. In each instance, teens are more likely to associate their social media use with generally positive rather than negative feelings. By relatively large margins, teens indicate that social media makes them feel included rather than excluded (71% vs. 25%), confident rather than insecure (69% vs. 26%), authentic rather than fake (64% vs. 33%) and outgoing rather than reserved (61% vs. 34%).

Interestingly, there are few demographic differences on these questions. For example, teen boys and girls are similarly likely to view their social media use in these ways, as are older and younger teens.

Better examples might take a look at the impact of cancel culture, cyberbullying or disinformation. By providing tangible examples that teens can relate to, educators can better draw comparisons and help teens understand the implications of much larger privacy issues, including protections and user rights. And of course, it helps to be authentic—which means understanding the appeal and dynamics of subcultures, trends and the collective power of creative communities.

Through collaboration and engagement, I believe a curriculum can be designed to emphasize safe and sustainable social media use and digital identity management. Hacks, identity theft, disinformation, misinformation and deep fakes are only going to increase in the coming decade. We need all users to help minimize the potential risks of our online lives, an initiative that can help protect my generation, their generation and future generations.

"Teens have never known a world without data sharing, and it's creating a false sense of security," by Ari Lightman, NBC News, January 15, 2021.

Roughly Four-in-Ten Teens Say They Regularly Unfriend or Unfollow People on Social Media—Citing Drama as Their Most Common Reason for Doing So

Just as relationships get forged and reinforced on social media, friendships can turn sour and require teens to prune their friend or follower lists. More than four-in-ten teens (44%) say they at least sometimes unfriend or unfollow people on social media, including 14% who say they do this often. But a somewhat larger share of teens say they engage in this behavior relatively sparingly. Just over half of young people report that they rarely (39%) or never (14%) unfriend or unfollow people on social media.

Teens who at least sometimes unfriend or unfollow people provide several reasons for deleting people from their friend lists on social media. But by far the most common reason (mentioned by 78% of teens who engage in this behavior) is that the person in question is simply creating too much drama.

In addition, more than half of these teens (54%) say they have unfriended or unfollowed someone because that person posted too much or too often, and a similar share disconnected from someone because the person bullied them or others.

A smaller share of these teens say they unfollow others because they act differently online than in person (43%) or post political views they disagree with (22%).

In general, girls are more active than boys at disconnecting from others on social media. Roughly half of girls (52%) say they at least sometimes unfriend or unfollow people, compared with 35% of boys. And girls are nearly twice as likely as boys to say they often unfriend or unfollow people on these platforms (18% vs. 10%). But among youth who do engage in this practice, boys and girls largely do so for similar reasons—with one exception. Boys are more likely than girls to say they've unfriended or unfollowed someone because that person posted too much or too often (67% of boys who regularly unfriend say this vs. 46% of girls).

Majorities of Teens Say Social Media Helps Them Find Different Points of View and Show Support for Causes, While Fewer Think of These Sites as a Source of Trustworthy Information

Majorities of teens believe social media helps people their age diversify their networks, broaden their viewpoints and get involved with issues they care about. Roughly two-thirds of teens say social networking sites helps teens at least some to interact with people from different backgrounds (69%), while a similar share credits social media with helping teens find different points of view (67%) or helping teens show their support for causes or issues (66%).

But much like older generations, relatively few teens think of social media platforms as a source of trustworthy information. Overall, 37% of teens think that social media helps people their age find trustworthy information—and only 7% think these sites help "a lot" in that respect.

Older teens are more likely than their younger peers to believe social media helps teens interact with people from various backgrounds. Fully 76% of 15-to 17-year-olds say this, compared with 59% of those ages 13 to 14. By a slightly lesser margin, older teens are more likely to say these platforms help people their age find diverse viewpoints (71% of older teens say this, vs. 60% of younger teens). Meanwhile, teens of all ages are similarly skeptical about social media's role as a source of trustworthy information.

Only Minorities of Teens Regularly Restrict Access to Their Social Media Posts to Prevent Parents or Other People from Seeing the Content

While some youth play an active role in controlling the content they see in their social media feeds and preventing various figures of authority from viewing what they post there, a large share of teens rarely curate their online presence in this way.

At a broad level, 46% of teens say they at least sometimes organize their feeds to only see certain types of content, although just 15% say they do this often. Indeed, 29% of teens say they never organize their social feeds in this way.

It is even rarer for teens to delete or restrict access to their posts because they might be seen by their parents or negatively impact them in the future. Just one-third of teens say they often or sometimes delete or restrict access to things they share on social media because they are concerned it could negatively impact them later in life. And about three-in-ten teens say they delete or restrict posts because they don't want their parents to view them. In both cases, only around one-in-ten young people say they do this often—and a plurality says they never do so.

There are also few demographic differences in deleting or restricting social media posts because it could negatively impact them in the future or because they don't want their parents to see what they've posted. But there are some age differences when it comes to taking steps to organize social media feeds. Older teens are more likely than their younger peers to say they regularly organize their feed in this way (51% of 15- to 17-year-olds do this vs. 37% of those ages 13 to 14).

Viewpoint 2

"Governments monitor every move you make to predict your behavior and control you better. And cybercriminals leave no stone unturned to steal your data for their nefarious purposes!"

Internet Privacy Should Be Zealously Guarded

Haris Shahid

In the following viewpoint, Haris Shahid declares internet privacy a basic human right, similar to the privacy people expect in their lives offline. But governments, companies, and cybercriminals are continuously attempting to enter into the private lives of internet users, both for legitimate and nefarious reasons. It is up to users to safeguard their private lives by taking steps to counter those who violate personal privacy. Shahid offers a number of actions one can take to have a safer internet experience. However, he warns, most users do little to ensure their online lives are not an open book. Haris Shahid is a software engineer and freelance writer who covers the latest happenings in the cybersecurity, privacy, and digital landscape.

As you read, consider the following questions:

1. What specific steps does Shahid suggest that will enable users to keep their online lives more private?
2. Which countries have the strictest privacy laws?
3. According to Shahid, why are web browsers not really free of cost?

The fact is that internet privacy has always mattered, whether it's 2010 or 2020. The only difference between the decade is that online threats and data breaches have escalated 10 times. That's not a good number nor a great time to be heading online without security measures.

Internet privacy is becoming a growing concern these days for people of all ages. Companies track your behavior across websites to serve you with highly relevant advertisements, making it essential for you to have an encrypted online connection—experience supreme AES 256-bit encryption with PureVPN.

Governments monitor every move you make to predict your behavior and control you better. And cybercriminals leave no stone unturned to steal your data for their nefarious purposes!

Instant connectivity has changed the way we live and work for the better, but this convenience comes at a huge price: your privacy*!* That's why it has become more important than ever for you to take responsibility for protecting your Internet privacy and personal information.

What is Internet Privacy?

Internet privacy, also commonly referred to as online privacy, is a subset of data privacy and a fundamental human right. Basically, it refers to the personal privacy that you're entitled to when you display, store, or provide information regarding yourself on the Internet.

This can include both personally-identifying information (PII) and non-personally-identifying information, such as your behavior on a website. Without Internet privacy, all your activities are subject to being collected and analyzed by interested parties!

3 Common Internet Privacy Issues to Watch Out For

Now that you understand what is Internet privacy and its importance, let's discuss the most common issues that surround your privacy online today:

1. Tracking

When you browse the Internet, you may have noticed those pesky ads following you where you go based on your earlier web searches or visits to websites. Well, that's because websites, advertisers, etc. track your movements.

Cookie profiling and other techniques are used to track your overall activities online and create a detailed profile of your browsing habits. Some people may not mind having relevant ads being served up to them, but this is a serious invasion of privacy for others.

2. Surveillance

Some governments spy on their citizens online to supposedly assist law enforcement agencies. For instance, the UK's Investigatory Powers Act authorizes mass surveillance and allows the government to monitor the Internet usage of its citizens legally.

Internet companies (ISPs), telcos, and other communication service providers are required to retain customers' Internet connection records for a year, which can be obtained by government authorities and used in investigations—even if you're not related to them in any way!

3. Theft

A staggering 17 million Americans were affected by identity theft in 2017, according to Javelin Strategy. Cybercriminals use malware, spyware, and phishing techniques to break into your online accounts or device and steal your personal information to engage in identity theft activities.

Of course, the victims end up losing most or all of their hard-earned money just because they didn't exercise caution when it comes to opening attachments, instant messages, or emails from unknown sources.

4 Internet Behaviors That Impact Your Privacy

You've heard time and time again that online privacy and security is important, but do you actually do something about it? Most of us practice bad Internet hygiene and don't even realize it, so don't forget to avoid doing the following:

1. Using the Same Credentials for Multiple Accounts

Sure, it's easy to remember and get things done online when you use the same credentials across your accounts. But if a cybercriminal can gain access to your one accounts, they'll most likely get into the other ones as well.

2. Staying Logged into Websites

Not logging out of websites and having them remember your credentials is indeed convenient. However, it also leaves your online accounts and personal information vulnerable to anyone who uses or hacks into your device.

3. Using Services without Reading their Terms & Conditions

Never click "agree" until you understand what you're getting yourself into. You wouldn't want to legally grant companies and service providers access to all kinds of data. Then sell this information to the highest bidder!

4. Opening Suspicious Attachments or Downloading Malicious Files

It would help if you were careful when opening attachments in emails or social media as they could contain malware and viruses. Similarly, it always downloads files from trusted sources because it may result in virus infection.

10 Ways to Protect Your Privacy and Security on the Internet

If you've made it this far, you've probably got a better idea of what Internet privacy concerns affect users. Now, you may be wondering, "how do I protect my privacy online?" Well, here are some measures that should be followed:

1. Secure Your Web Browser

Your browser is the main program you use to go online, so make sure you take the necessary steps to secure it. After all, cybercriminals can take advantage of loopholes in browsers to access the personal data on your device. To protect your online privacy and security, we'd recommend that you follow the recommendations in our ultimate browser security guide.

2. Use a Virtual Private Network (VPN)

Using a VPN is the best way to protect your Internet privacy. Not only does it change your IP address and assign you a new one based on the VPN server you're connected to, but it also protects your incoming and outgoing traffic with military-grade encryption.

As a result, your online activities and personal information stay secure and private from snoopers. PureVPN is regarded as the best VPN when it comes to online privacy and security, and for all the right reasons.

3. Keep Your Software Up-to-Date

If you leave vulnerabilities in your software, the chances are that the bad guys will exploit them! Keep your operating system, browser, and other software (like Adobe Flash and Java) up to date to ensure that you don't miss out on new features and security fixes. If you find it a hassle to apply updates manually, you can always use tools to automate your software updates.

4. Install an Anti-virus Program & Activate Firewall

You can keep your safe from harmful content on the Internet with a few simple precautions. A strong anti-virus program will keep your device free from all types of malware, such as spyware, viruses, Trojans, etc. You should also activate your firewall to keep unwanted network traffic at bay. The good news is that most operating systems come with it built-in.

5. Delete Cookies at Browser Exit

You should delete cookies regularly as they're used by websites, advertisers, and other third parties to track you online. While you can clear your cookies manually, you're better off configuring your browser to delete them at the end of the browsing session automatically. If you don't know how to, follow our guide to deleting browsing cookies automatically at browser exit.

6. Adjust Your Settings on Google, Facebook, etc.

Take advantage of the options that are available to you. Big Internet companies such as Facebook and Google usually give you options to opt-out of some, if not all, of their personalization and tracking. For example, you can manage your ads preferences on Facebook from here, while Google allows you to turn off ad personalization.

7. Use HTTPS to Secure Your Online Connection

If you are on a website that uses HTTPS, likely, any personal data flowing between you and the website is probably being monitored by trackers or potentially intercepted and stolen by malicious hackers. These entities are commonly referred to as man-in-the-middle.

An HTTPS or Secure Sockets Layer (SSL) encrypts your online communication with that website. If you are on any website, especially a shopping website, you should ensure that you have an HTTPS connection. For the utmost online privacy and security, you should resort to a VPN service.

8. Defuse Threats When Backing up to the Cloud

In today's era, we constantly back up our pictures and other files on the cloud. Backing up on the cloud comes packed with its own privacy issues. Anyone could intercept your internet connection and view the data you are backing up or downloading from the cloud.

To defuse this threat, it's advised that you use state-of-the-art AES 256-bit encryption that will secure your internet connection, meaning you can download and upload sensitive information without worrying about anyone tapping in on your private data.

9. Secure Online Communications

Most of your online communications platforms are unsecure. While numerous messaging apps offer end-to-end encryption, security experts advise adding a layer of encryption to your online communication.

As far as emails and messaging on chat apps are concerned, it would help if you opted for reputable services such as Signal, Telegram, etc. When it comes to emails, use secure mail services.

10. Share Online Files Securely

Securely share files with anyone on the web by password protecting them. With a password protecting your PDF or any other file, you can rest assured that the intended recipient only views it.

11.Use Multi Factor Authentication

Multi-factor Authentication (MFA) or Two-factor Authentication (2FA) is an added authentication method apart from the conventional password. The intent of this step is so that the user provides more than one way to gain access to their online account, application or any other software that supports multi-factor authentication.

With multi-factor authentication enabled, you significantly reduce the chances of your account getting sabotaged or falling victim to a cyberattack.

Internet Privacy FAQs

The following are answers to some of the most frequently asked questions about Internet privacy:

Is Internet Privacy Dead?

Yes, it sure does seem that way. Every time you browse the Internet, your privacy is under constant threat from cybercriminals, governments, and corporations who want to get their hands on your personal information. That's exactly why it's up to each one of us to protect our privacy and personal space on the Internet.

Why Does Internet Privacy Matter?

Take a second and imagine a world without privacy on the Internet, where all your activities and personal information such as medical records, bank balances, credit card information, and emails exist out in the plain open for *anyone* to see.

Still, think you have nothing to hide? Probably not. Privacy matters because, without it, the Internet becomes a less safe place for us to indulge in. After all, there would be nothing stopping what you do online from being entirely public.

Will the Desire for Internet Privacy Gradually Decrease?

The desire for privacy on the Internet is only going to increase with time. Why? Because our online activities are always being tracked and recorded by somebody—whether it's the ISP, big internet companies like Google and Facebook, or government bodies.

As such, more and more Internet users realize the importance of protecting their privacy and personal data. This is evident from the fact that there has been significant growth in the use of VPNs and other anonymizing technologies over the last few years.

What Countries Have the Toughest Internet Privacy Laws?

According to Privacy International, the following countries rank in the top 5 of the Privacy Index, meaning they give their citizens the least protection in terms of Internet privacy:

England

Singapore
Russia
Malaysia
China
Learn more about internet privacy laws in certain countries here.

What Are Some Interesting Facts Internet Privacy?

Here are a few important facts about Internet privacy that you should understand:

1. While many social media sites and search engines can be used free of cost, they often come at the cost of your Internet privacy as they track your browsing history and sell it to the highest bidder or use that information to show you targeted advertisements.
2. Private browsing doesn't protect your privacy from entities that monitor your activities on the Internet. It only prevents your browser from recording information about you—third-parties can pretty much still see what you're up to online.
3. Everything you do, and everywhere you go online has already been saved and archived by your ISP. Since they assign your IP address, your Internet traffic (what websites you're visiting, which apps you're using, etc.) can be seen by them as it goes through their servers.

How to Secure Your Internet Browsing Activities

To secure your internet browsing activities, you'll need to protect your internet connection by employing AES 256-bit encryption. Encryption secures your online activities by encoding your data, keeping you safe from eavesdroppers.

What Is the Biggest Threat to Internet Privacy?

The biggest threat to internet privacy in our digital age is humans. Internet users use weak passwords, click on phishing emails and, most importantly, use an unsecured internet connection. To stay away from online threats, start encrypting your online activities.

Final Word

Privacy on the Internet is your basic right, and you need to fight for it! By incorporating these Internet privacy tips into your daily lives, you'll be able to protect your privacy online and browse with peace of mind, knowing that your personal information won't fall into the wrong hands.

Resources

1. The Verge, "How to increase your privacy online," by Jacob Kastrenakes on Thursday, June 7, 2018.
2. The Next Web, "7 ways to protect your privacy on the internet," by Morgan Slain on Tuesday, August 18, 2015.

VIEWPOINT 3

> *"Think back to when you were in high school and imagine the most embarrassing thing that happened to you in a classroom. Now imagine a recording of that being made and shared in a format that potentially ensures it will live there forever."*

Schools Must Protect the Privacy of Their Students

Sydney Johnson

In the following viewpoint, Sydney Johnson writes of the dangers involved as more and more schools transfer to online learning, during and after the coronavirus pandemic. Laws are already in place to protect student privacy, and schools must follow these laws. When giving lessons on platforms such as Zoom, teachers must be careful to follow federal and state laws pertaining to student privacy. These laws can be complicated, and it is best to use software platforms that have been vetted by school districts. Sydney Johnson covers math and science, among other topics, for EdSource. Her work has also appeared in Slate, The Huffington Post, the East Bay Express, San Francisco magazine and other outlets.

"Quick Guide: How to Protect a Student's Privacy Online," by Sydney Johnson, EdSource, April 29, 2020. Reprinted by permission.

As you read, consider the following questions:

1. What does federal law say about collecting personal information about children under 13?
2. What does the law say about teens 13 to 16?
3. What is "zoombombing" and how can teachers protect against it?

As California schools hurry to implement distance learning plans for students at home during the coronavirus pandemic, many are facing new questions about how to protect student data privacy as they shift to online education. Here's what parents, educators and students need to know:

What Privacy Laws Apply to California Students?

In 2014, California passed the Student Online Personal Information Protection Act, which prohibits companies providing online services for K-12 schools and students from selling student data or using that information to advertise to students. It also requires that companies delete student data if a school or district requests it.

That law aligned with federal student privacy laws, including the Children's Online Privacy Act, which applies to online businesses that sell products or services for children. Enacted in 1998, the law requires a website or mobile app to obtain parental consent before it can collect personal information about children under 13. It also requires the site or app to disclose their data collection practices, such as in an online privacy policy.

The new California Consumer Privacy Act applies to data collected by non-education apps that teachers might use during the pandemic, such as Zoom. The law extends requirements for collecting, selling and deleting personal information to companies providing all types of services—not just those that are aimed at children. It also requires those companies to obtain a parent's permission before selling personal data of a child under 13. Teens between the ages of 13 and 16 can give consent themselves.

The new consumer privacy act lists education records, as defined under the federal Family Educational Rights and Privacy Act, as personal information and gives students over 16 in high school and college the right to opt out of the sale of their data.

Can Teachers Use Video with Students if Teaching Remotely?

Yes—but be careful. There generally aren't privacy issues with a teacher giving a video lesson. And it can be comforting for some students and easier to learn from a familiar face on screen rather than a recorded voice or worksheet.

But schools can run into problems if teachers or students record or snap photos of the virtual classroom.

"Think back to when you were in high school and imagine the most embarrassing thing that happened to you in a classroom," said Bill Fitzgerald, a Consumer Reports privacy researcher. "Now imagine a recording of that being made and shared in a format that potentially ensures it will live there forever."

A safe alternative is for teachers to stick to a lecture or short video lessons and don't record the parts that involve students if possible, said Amelia Vance, director of education privacy at the Future of Privacy Forum, a nonprofit think tank that focuses on data privacy.

Fitzgerald suggests strategies like student-led research or one-on-one check-ins with a teacher and student that don't require a class to attend a video meeting.

Can Teachers Share Photos of Virtual Classes Online?

No, Vance said. Photos of students, as well as their names, which often appear on their video in a video conference platform, are personal information and privacy laws apply, she said.

How Do Teachers Prevent Inappropriate Screen Shares or Zoombombing?

One of the simplest ways to avoid unwanted video guests or screen shares, now commonly referred to as Zoombombing, is by using the security settings that are available to those who are hosts in a meeting. Those settings include who can determine who has access to the meeting and who can control the screen.

To keep uninvited attendees out, teachers can check to see if their video service allows for password-protected meetings so others can't join in if they find (or guess) the meeting ID number. Zoom recently updated its video settings to require a password by default to enter a meeting. The password settings are locked for free K-12 education Zoom accounts and cannot be turned off.

Another important tip: Schools should set expectations early, such as making it clear that using a cell phone to take a video of an in-class video session is a violation of school policy.

How Can I Check if the Tools Being Used by a School Will Protect Students' Data Privacy?

Teachers should try to stick to education technology products that districts have vetted for privacy already, Vance said. If that's not possible, companies that collect personally identifiable information—such as email addresses, Social Security numbers, or education records—must have a public-facing privacy policy that users can review.

When using tools like Zoom, teachers should avoid creating consumer accounts and instead open an education account, which has a different privacy policy for student data. Zoom handles personal data of K-12 school accounts differently than basic accounts, but says both privacy policies are compliant with privacy laws.

"Educators who sign up separately from the education product are subjecting themselves and the students to the normal policy," Vance said. "A lot of virtual classrooms are being created where we don't know how the data is being shared or sold or other things that are highly regulated under student privacy laws."

Common Sense Media also publishes free reviews of education and children's apps with ratings on how well a company's privacy policy aligns with federal and state student data privacy laws, as well as how transparent and strong the policy is.

The California County Superintendents Educational Services Association has created a sample checklist and other guidance for school districts on complying with the student online privacy laws.

How Can Parents Ask Companies to Delete or Stop Selling Their Child's Data?

In California, companies are required to offer at least two ways for consumers to request to know what data companies collect about them, ask for it to be deleted and opt out of the sale of their data for users over 16. Options might include a "Do Not Sell My Info" link on a business' website, a toll-free number or a direct email address.

Common Sense Media has forms for parents and consumers to ask companies to stop selling their or their children's data.

If a third-party education company stores student data in the cloud, parents should contact the school or district to make a request to the vendor to delete student data.

What Are Some Limitations in California's Privacy Laws?

While compliance with privacy policies is important, Fitzgerald said it's "the lowest bar" to ensuring students have a safe and meaningful learning experience. "A company can be fully compliant and still not do great things with data," such as collecting and storing non-essential information about users.

Another issue is simply raising awareness of the rights that California parents and students have regarding their data. Some may not know it is up to a user to request that their information be deleted or to request their data to stop being sold if the user is over 16. Another issue is that opting out can be a burden, as most students and families use a number of different apps and digital tools they would have to contact individually.

Viewpoint 4

> *"The scams include the rapidly growing phenomenon of 'money mules,' where thousands of young people are being coerced by criminals into laundering the proceeds of crime through their bank accounts."*

Teens Are Being Scammed on Social Media

Mark White

In the following viewpoint, Mark White explores how teenagers on social media are being used by scammers to launder money. Innocent teenagers who are seeking a quick buck are targeted by older, more sophisticated scammers who gain access to their bank accounts for nefarious purposes. It is clear that there is no such thing as free money, White warns, and teenagers should run away quickly from schemes that look too good to be true. Mark White is Home Affairs Correspondent for Sky News, a British publication.

As you read, consider the following questions:

1. Why, according to "Fraudster Dan," are social media scammers free to steal with impunity?
2. How does the scheme of using a money mule work?
3. Why are young people so susceptible to scams, according to the viewpoint?

"Revealed: How fraudsters are scamming teenage 'money mules' on Instagram and Snapchat," by Mark White, Sky News, February 8, 2019. Reprinted by permission.

Fraudsters are able to operate with impunity on social media networks like Instagram and Snapchat, scamming users and running little risk of being caught, a Sky News investigation has found.

Police and anti-fraud groups are also warning that a too-trusting Instagram generation is falling victim to get-rich-quick scams, worth many millions of pounds a year to criminals.

Figures obtained by Sky News show under 25s are six times more likely to fall victim to criminals using social media platforms than over 50s.

The scams include the rapidly growing phenomenon of "money mules", where thousands of young people are being coerced by criminals into laundering the proceeds of crime through their bank accounts.

Fraudsters entice their victims with the prospect of a share of the money being laundered, but much of the time they receive nothing.

Not Savvy Enough

Being ultra-tech-savvy apparently isn't enough to protect you from online scams, a new report suggests.

The number of individuals age 20 or younger—members of Generation Z who have grown up on smartphones and the internet—reporting they are victims of cyber-fraud has surged 156% over the last three years, according to a study from Social Catfish, an online identity-verification service. That compares to 112% growth during the same time among people age 60 or older, the group with the next-fastest scam growth.

"It is alarming," said David McClellan, president of Social Catfish. "The generation we think of as being the most savvy with the internet ... is where the numbers are growing the fastest when it comes to scams."

A recent Europe-wide crackdown by law enforcement agencies prevented around £31m in illegal transactions by around 1,500 money mules.

Many victims are also tricked into handing over details of their bank accounts and other personal information to the criminals, who then raid their accounts or make financial transactions using those stolen details.

Dan, from north London, has been scamming social media users for several years.

"They want to make easy money. They just think they're handing over a bank card with their details," he said.

"They don't realise they're not going to see any of this money at the end of it."

Dan said neither he nor any of his friends carrying out similar scams have ever been caught.

He said online media companies and the police never seem interested in pursuing offenders.

> For the under-21 crowd, complaints to the FBI's Internet Crime Complaint Center reached about 23,200 last year (up from 9,000 in 2017), resulting in roughly $71 million lost (compared with $8.3 million in 2017).
>
> "This age group is very comfortable being online and being very public about their lives," McClellan said. "So that makes them very trusting when they're on the Internet."
>
> While the growth in complaints was fastest for the nation's youngest generation, more older Americans are victimized overall: Last year, 105,300 or so complaints of online scams among those age 60 or older resulted in a collective $966 million loss, the study says.
>
> Overall, victims of all ages collectively lost $4.2 billion in 2020, according to an FBI report, which the Social Catfish study relied on as part of its research.
>
> **"Tech-savvy Teens Falling Prey to Online Scams Faster than Their Grandparents," by Sarah O'Brien, CNBC, August 10, 2021.**

Across the internet, particularly on social media, temptation is everywhere. These are glamorous looking accounts offering get-rich-quick schemes.

The ads claim "it's easy money" and according to Dan there is no shortage of people, particularly the young, willing to take the risk.

"The easiest way now is to go on Instagram and type in 'instant cash' or something like that," he said

"There's so many following these groups, advertising the exact same thing you are. There are thousands who want to get rich.

"You just drop them a line saying 'do you want to make easy cash? - have you got a card?' and you're quickly inundated with lots of takers."

Dan's assertion is borne out by the latest figures from leading fraud prevention agency Cifas.

They show that between January and October last year, around 30,000 money mules were identified in the UK—around a third were aged under 21 and almost 5,000 were younger than 18.

Rochelle was just 15 when she was approached on Instagram and offered the chance to become a money mule.

As a young teenager, she had no money and the offer of a few hundred pounds for sharing her bank details seemed too good to resist.

But it was a scam. Money was laundered through her account, but quickly withdrawn again and she got nothing from the criminal gang.

The bank later questioned her and blocked her account.

"I felt really humiliated, because I can't believe I actually thought that I was going to get this money," she said.

"I think people are actually afraid to say that it hasn't worked, because they feel humiliated and embarrassed.

"I know my sibling got scammed, my best friend got scammed and a lot of my other friends got scammed."

Social media companies have been accused of doing little to stop criminals exploiting their networks.

Instagram said: “Criminal activity is not allowed on Instagram and our community guidelines clearly state that people must follow the law. We encourage people to report content they think is against our guidelines using our in-app tools.”

UK banks are being more proactive, joining forces and using sophisticated computer algorithms to pin-point fraudulent activity.

Tony Blake, head of fraud prevention for UK Finance, said: “The ultimate aim is to stop the money going in, to freeze that money and hopefully repatriate it, if possible.

“We obviously also want to close those accounts and stop those people opening accounts in the first place.”

The police have told Sky News they will pursue those involved in trying to launder money through the banking network.

In October 2018, Michael Lanyuru, 24, from east London, was jailed for 21 months for laundering cash through money mules.

Acting detective inspector Paul Curtis, from the financial investigation unit at the City of London Police, urged social media users to adopt a common sense approach when faced with tempting online offers.

“Ultimately, there is no free money. If somebody is asking to use your account for a fee, that is illegal.

“You have to make sure you know where the money is coming from and if you can’t account for it, you do risk prosecution for money laundering.”

Fraudster Dan said he believes the risk of being caught is negligible and he plans to keep on committing online crime as long as there are willing victims.

“If you keep going online and you keep seeing these accounts with 7,000 people on it.. that’s like 7,000 potential people that would willingly hand over their bank card. Once they hand over their bank card, that’s it.”

VIEWPOINT 5

"Privacy isn't about being isolated from others. It's about having the capacity to control a social situation."

Parents Should Not Panic About Teens' Social Media Habits

Brian Bergstein

In the following viewpoint Brian Bergstein interviews Microsoft researcher Danah Boyd to discuss how social media is not quite the all-encompassing evil that many have made it out to be. Previous generations of teens were able to roam much more freely than they are today, in a society where parents are afraid to let their children just go outside. Consequently, teens congregate online, and their online lives are not much different from teens' lives in previous generations. Teens are much more concerned about their privacy than their parents give them credit for, and they know how to control their online lives, Boyd states. Brian Bergstein has been a technology journalist since 2000, reporting from Silicon Valley, New York, and Boston. He is currently the Deputy Opinion Editor of the Boston Globe.

As you read, consider the following questions:

1. What were Boyd's surprising findings regarding bullying?
2. What, according to Boyd, should parents be doing to help teens navigate the pitfalls of social media?

"Parents: Don't Panic About Your Kids' Social Media Habits," by Brian Bergstein, MIT Technology Review, December 12, 2013. Reprinted by permission.

3. What does Boyd say today's teens will someday worry about with their own children?

Kids today! They're online all the time, sharing every little aspect of their lives. What's wrong with them? Actually, nothing, says Danah Boyd, a Microsoft researcher who studies social media. In a book coming out this winter, It's Complicated: The Social Lives of Networked Teens, Boyd argues that teenagers aren't doing much online that's very different from what kids did at the sock hop, the roller rink, or the mall. They do so much socializing online mostly because they have little choice, Boyd says: parents now generally consider it unsafe to let kids roam their neighborhoods unsupervised. Boyd, 36, spoke with MIT Technology Review's deputy editor, Brian Bergstein, at Microsoft Research's offices in Manhattan.

I feel like you might have titled the book Everybody Should Stop Freaking Out.

It's funny, because one of the early titles was Like, Duh. Because whenever I would show my research to young people, they'd say, "Like, duh. Isn't this so obvious?" And it opens with the anecdote of a boy who says, "Can you just talk to my mom? Can you tell her that I'm going to be okay?" I found that refrain so common among young people.

You and your colleague Alice Marwick interviewed 166 teenagers for this book. But you've studied social media for a long time. What surprised you?

It was shocking how heavily constrained their mobility was. I had known it had gotten worse since I was a teenager, but I didn't get it—the total lack of freedom to just go out and wander. Young people weren't even trying to sneak out [of the house at night]. They were trying to get online, because that's the place where they hung out with their friends.

And I had assumed based on the narratives in the media that bullying was on the rise. I was shocked that data showed otherwise.

Then why do narratives such as "Bullying is more common online" take hold?

It's made more visible. There is some awful stuff out there, but it frustrates me when a panic distracts us from the reality of what's going on. One of my frustrations is that there are some massive mental health issues, and we want to blame the technology [that brings them to light] instead of actually dealing with mental health issues.

I take your point that Facebook or Instagram is the equivalent of yesterday's hangouts. But social media amplify everyday situations in difficult new ways. For example, kids might instantly see on Facebook that they're missing out on something other kids are doing together.

That can be a blessing or a curse. These interpersonal conflicts ramp up much faster [and] can be much more hurtful. That's one of the challenges for this cohort of youth: some of them have the social and emotional skills that are necessary to deal with these conflicts; others don't. It really sucks when you realize that somebody doesn't like you as much as you like them. Part of it is, then, how do you use that as an opportunity not to just wallow in your self-pity but to figure out how to interact and be like "Hey, let's talk through what this friendship is like"?

You contend that teenagers are not cavalier about privacy, despite appearances, and adeptly shift sensitive conversations into chat and other private channels.

Many adults assume teens don't care about privacy because they're so willing to participate in social media. They want to be in public. But that doesn't mean that they want to be public. There's a big difference. Privacy isn't about being isolated from others. It's about having the capacity to control a social situation.

So if parents can let go of some common fears, what should they be doing?

One thing that I think is dangerous is that we're trained that we are the experts at everything that goes on in our lives and our kids' lives. So the assumption is that we should teach them by telling them. But I think the best way to teach is by asking questions: "Why are you posting that? Help me understand." Using it as an opportunity to talk. Obviously there comes a point when your teenage child is going to roll their eyes and go, "I am not interested in explaining anything more to you, Dad."

The other thing is being present. The hardest thing that I saw, overwhelmingly—the most unhealthy environments—were those where the parents were not present. They could be physically present and not actually present.

What will today's teenagers worry about with their kids?

The core concerns tend not to change: sexuality and the display of sexuality. For me it was leather miniskirts, and the ridiculous bangs, and fishnets, and bras on top of your shirts—gasp! Today it's sexting and selfies. And pressures for freedom: over generations we keep finding new ways to constrain and control, and technologies provide a relief valve or a way of getting around them. All of a sudden there's a new form of freedom.

Periodical and Internet Sources Bibliography

The following articles have been selected to supplement the diverse views presented in this chapter.

The Bark Team, "Teaching Your Child About Social Media and Privacy Online" Bark. February 16, 2022. https://www.bark.us/blog/social-media-privacy/.

Vivian Ho, "Facebook's privacy problems: a roundup," *Guardian*. December 13, 2018. https://www.theguardian.com/technology/2018/dec/14/facebook-privacy-problems-roundup.

Rosie Hopegood, "The perils of 'sharenting': The parents who share too much," Al Jazeera. October 11, 2020. https://www.aljazeera.com/features/2020/10/11/facing-the-music-the-parents-who-share-too-much.

Hua Hsu, "Instagram, Facebook, and the Perils of 'Sharenting.'" *New Yorker*. September 11, 2019. https://www.newyorker.com/culture/cultural-comment/instagram-facebook-and-the-perils-of-sharenting.

Carolyn Jones, "Is crackdown on social media for kids too late?," Edsource. March 16, 2022. https://edsource.org/2022/citing-the-impact-on-children-officials-ramp-up-efforts-to-regulate-social-media/668911.

Suren Ramasubbu, "Privacy and Teens in Social Media," The Huffington Post. March 3, 2017. https://www.huffpost.com/entry/privacy-and-teens-in-social-media_b_58b92d56e4b0fa65b844b1de.

Rachel Siemens, "3 Teenagers on How It Feels to Grow Up with Social Media," repeller. Aug. 20, 2018. https://repeller.com/teenagers-privacy-social-media/.

Denise Witmer, "Why Teens Need Privacy from Their Parents," Verywell Family. March 27, 2022. https://www.verywellfamily.com/why-does-my-teen-need-privacy-2609615.

For Further Discussion

Chapter 1

1. After reading the viewpoints in this chapter, do you believe that social media use endangers teens' mental health, or are these concerns overblown?
2. After reading the viewpoints by Christie and Goodyear and Quennerstedt, how do you think social media is beneficial to teens?
3. After reading the viewpoints in this chapter, what are some ways to avoid letting social media harm one's mental health?

Chapter 2

1. Based on the viewpoints in this chapter, who do you believe should be primarily responsible for protecting teens online?
2. Many of the viewpoints in this chapter put the onus for protecting teens squarely on their parents. Do you think this is fair? Why or why not?
3. Do you think users should be able to sue social media platforms such as Facebook and Instagram for causing mental distress or even suicide? Cite examples from this chapter to support your answer.

Chapter 3

1. After reading the viewpoints in this chapter, how serious a threat do you believe cyberbullying in social media is?
2. Do you believe that cyberbullying laws should be strengthened?
3. After reading the viewpoints in this chapter, do you believe that cyberbullying is worse than traditional bullying or is it just more of the same?

Chapter 4

1. Do you think teen privacy is in jeopardy on social media? Why or why not?
2. What is your opinion on the practice of "sharenting" teen information on social media?
3. Do you believe that parents need to snoop on their teens' social media behavior to keep them safe online? Why or why not?

Organizations to Contact

The editors have compiled the following list of organizations concerned with the issues debated in this book. The descriptions are derived from materials provided by the organizations. All have publications or information available for interested readers. The list was compiled on the date of publication of the present volume; the information provided here may change. Be aware that many organizations take several weeks or longer to respond to inquiries, so allow as much time as possible.

Berkman Klein Center for Internet & Society

1557 Massachusetts Avenue, 5th Floor,
Cambridge MA 02138
(617) 495-7547
email: cyber@law.harvard.edu
website: http://cyber.law.harvard.edu

The Berkman Klein Center's mission is to explore and understand cyberspace; to study its development, dynamics, norms, and standards; and to assess the need or lack thereof for laws and sanctions. They are a research center, premised on the observation that what they seek to learn is not already recorded. Their method is to build out into cyberspace, record data as they go, self-study, and share. Their mode is entrepreneurial nonprofit. Their website offers publications such as *Youth and Extended Reality* and *Youth and Cyberbullying*.

Center for Democracy & Technology

1401 K Street NW, Suite 200
Washington, D.C. 20005
(202) 637-9800
website: https://cdt.org

CDT works to promote democratic values by shaping technology policy and architecture, with a focus on the rights of the individual. They champion policies, laws, and technical designs that empower people to use technology for good while protecting against invasive, discriminatory, and exploitative uses. They work to ensure that online platforms are transparent, accountable, and respect human rights. They believe regulation should set limits on the collection and use of personal information and give people greater control. A searchable database reveals articles such as "States Take Steps to Limit School Surveillance of Student Social Media Pages" and "Protecting Student Privacy in the Race to Close the Homework Gap."

Common Sense Media

699 8th St, Suite C150
San Francisco, CA 94103
(415) 863-0600
website: www.commonsensemedia.org

Common Sense is an independent voice for kids, families, and communities everywhere. They combine original research with game-changing advocacy efforts to make the digital world work better for all young people. Their advocacy work highlights legislation related to technology and identifies solutions that protect consumer privacy, push for better connectivity for students and families, and hold tech companies accountable to ensure a healthy internet for all. Their website contains research reports such as The *Common Sense Census: Media Use by Tweens and Teens, 2021* and *Tweens, Teens, Tech, and Mental Health: Coming of Age in an Increasingly Digital, Uncertain, and Unequal World, 2020.*

The Federal Trade Commission (FTC)

600 Pennsylvania Avenue, NW
Washington, DC 20580
(202) 326-2222
website: www.ftc.gov

The FTC's mission is to protect consumers and competition by preventing anticompetitive, deceptive, and unfair business practices through law enforcement, advocacy, and education without unduly burdening legitimate business activity. Their work to protect consumers and promote competition touches the economic life of every American. They are the only federal agency that deals with consumer protection and competition issues in broad sectors of the economy. Evidence of their work in protecting Americans from deceptive trade practices can be seen on their website in the form of releases such as "FTC Issues Orders to Nine Social Media and Video Streaming Services Seeking Data About How They Collect, Use, and Present Information."

Internet Keep Safe Coalition

601 New Jersey Avenue NW
Suite 350
Washington, DC 20001
(202) 505-4408
email: info@ikeepsafe.org
website: ikeepsafe.org

The iKeepSafe mission is to provide a safe digital landscape for children, schools, and families by supporting the protection of student privacy, while advancing learning in a digital culture. To support this mission, we provide data privacy certifications to technology companies, educational resources to schools, and information to the community.

Internet Society (ISOC)

11710 Plaza America Drive
Suite 400
Reston, VA 20190
(703) 439-2120
email: isoc@isoc.org
website: www.internetsociety.org

The Internet Society supports and promotes the development of the Internet as a global technical infrastructure, a resource to enrich people's lives, and a force for good in society. Their work aligns with their goals for the Internet to be open, globally connected, secure, and trustworthy. They seek collaboration with all who share these goals.The Internet Society focuses on: building and supporting the communities that make the internet work; advancing the development and application of internet infrastructure, technologies, and open standards; and advocating for policy that is consistent with their view of the Internet. They produce reports such as "Children and the Internet," available for download at their website.

National Center on Safe Supportive Learning Environments

1400 Crystal Drive, 10th Floor
Arlington, VA 22202-3289
(800) 258.8413 |
email: ncssle@air.org
website: safesupportivelearning.ed.gov

The National Center on Safe Supportive Learning environments sponsors The Cyberbullying Research Center, which serves as a clearinghouse of information concerning the ways adolescents use and misuse technology geared toward parents, educators, law enforcement officers, counselors, and others who work with youth. The site, at cyberbullying.org includes figures and detailed stories from those who have been directly impacted by online aggression and includes numerous resources to help users prevent and respond to cyberbullying incidents.

National Cybersecurity Alliance

1010 Vermont Ave Nw # 821
Washington, DC 20005
(202)570-7430
email: info@staysafeonline.org

website: staysafeonline.org

The National Cybersecurity Alliance is a non-profit organization whose mission is to create a more secure, interconnected world. They advocate for the safe use of all technology and educate users about how best to protect ourselves, their families, and their organizations from cybercrime. They create strong partnerships between governments and corporations to amplify their message and to foster a greater "digital" good. The Stay Safe Online section of their website has features on cyberbullying, internet privacy, safety measures for the LGBTQ community, and more.

Pew Research Center

1615 L St. NW, Suite 800
Washington, DC 20036 USA
(202) 419-4300
website: www.pewinternet.org

Pew Research Center is a nonpartisan fact tank that informs the public about the issues, attitudes and trends shaping the world. They conduct public opinion polling, demographic research, content analysis and other data-driven social science research. They do not take policy positions. Their website contains a section on Internet and Technology that is full of relevant articles and polls.

WiredSafety

227 S New York Ave
Wellston, Ohio, 45692,
(201) 463-8663
website: www.wiredsafety.com

WiredSafety was the first online safety, education, and help group in the world. Originating in 1995 as a group of volunteers rating websites and helping victims of cyberharassment, it now provides one-to-one help, resources and extensive information, and education to cyberspace users of all ages on a myriad of Internet and interactive technology safety, privacy and security comprised entirely of unpaid volunteers who administer specialized websites, resources and programs. WiredSafety's programs and sites include StopCyberbullying.org, POSTitPositive.com, WiredCops.org, Teenangels.org, and Tweenangels.org. Their website includes information on cyberbullying, online safety, privacy, and more.

Bibliography of Books

Danah Boyd. *It's Complicated: The Social Lives of Networked Teens*. New Haven: Yale Univ. Press, 2015.

Kaitlyn Duling. *Social Media and Digitial Stress*. Minneapolis, MN: Essential Library, 2022.

Claire Edwards. *Social Media and Mental Health: Handbook for Teens*. Nottinghamshire, England: Trigger, 2018.

Sherri M. Gordon. *Weaponized Social Media*. New York: Enslow Publishing, 2019.

Christine Greenhow, Julia Sonnevend, and Colin Agur. *Education and Social Media: Toward a Digital Future*. Cambridge, MA: The MIT Press, 2016.

Bonnie Hinman. *Teens and Social Media*, San Diego: Reference Point Press, 2019.

Ana Homayoun. *Social Media Wellness: Helping Tweens and Teens Thrive in an Unbalanced Digital World*. Thousand Oaks, California: Corwin, a Sage Company, 2018.

Mizuko Ito, Sonja Baumer, Matteo Bittanti, Danah Boyd, Rachel Cody, Becky Herr-Stephenson, Heather A. Horst, Patricia G. Lange, Dilan Mahendran, Katynka Z. Martinez, C J. Pascoe, Dan Perkel, Laura Robinson, Christo Sims, and Lisa M. Tripp. *Hanging Out, Messing Around, and Geeking Out: Kids Living and Learning with New Media*. Cambridge MA: M.I.T. Press, 2019.

Thomas A. Jacobs. *Cyberbullying Law*. Chicago, Illinois: American Bar Association, 2020.

Mary Madden. *Teens, Social Media, and Privacy*. Washington, D.C: Pew Research Center, Washington, D.C.: Pew Research Center, 2013.

Gwenn S. O'Keeffe. *Cybersafe: Protecting and Empowering Kids in the Digital World of Texting, Gaming, and Social Media*. Elk Grove Village, Ill: American Academy of Pediatrics, 2011.

Deana Puccio and Allison Havey. *Sex, Likes and Social Media: How the Digital Age Is Affecting Our Teens—and What We Can Do to Help*. London: Vermillion, 2016.

Aimee Rickman. *Adolescence, Girlhood, and Media Migration: Us Teens' Use of Social Media to Negotiate Offline Struggles.* Lanham, MD: Lexington Books, 2018.

Lauri S. Scherer. *Cyberbullying*. Farmington Hills, MI: Greenhaven Press, 2015.

Heather E. Schwartz. *Cyberbullying*. Capstone Global Library Ltd, 2017.

Smith, Stephen J. *Social Media & The Adolescent Digital Tribe: Navigating the Teen World State*. Publisher Services, 2019.

Ungvarsky, Janine. *The Risks of Social Media*. San Diego, CA: BrightPoint Press, 2022.

Jill Walsh. *Adolescents and Their Social Media Narratives: A Digital Coming of Age*. London: Routledge, Taylor & Francis Group, 2018.

Index

E

F

G

H

I

J

K

L

M

P

Q

R

T

U

V

W

Y

Z